BOY SOLDIERS
OF THE CONFEDERACY

BOY SOLDIERS OF THE CONFEDERACY

COLLATED BY

SUSAN R. HULL

ILLUSTRATED BY PORTRAITS

EAKIN PRESS ★ Austin, TX

Published in the United States of America
By Eakin Press
An Imprint of Sunbelt Media, Inc.
P. O. Drawer 90159 ★ Austin, Texas 78709-0159

2 3 4 5 6 7 8 9

ISBN 1-57168-229-5

Library of Congress Cataloging-in-Publication Data

Hull, Susan R., b. 1833.
Boy soldiers of the Confederacy / collated by Susan R. Hull.
p. cm.
Originally published: New York : Neale Pub. Co., 1905.
Includes index.
ISBN 1-57168-229-5
1. United States--History--Civil War, 1881-1865--Participation, Juvenile. 2. Boys as soldiers--Confederate States of America--History. 3. Boys as soldiers--Confederate States of America--Biography. I. Title.
E585.C54H85 1998
973.7'08054--dc21 98-10629
CIP

TO

Lt.-Col. John Baker Thompson

of the "Magnificent First Arkansas," C.S.A.

"Let laurels, drench'd in pure Parnassian dews,
Reward his mem'ry, dear to ev'ry muse,
Who, with a courage of unshaken root,
In honour's field advancing his firm foot,
Plants it upon the line that justice draws,
And will prevail or perish in her cause.
'Tis to the virtues of such men, man owes
His portion in the good that Heav'n bestows.
And when recording history displays
Feats of renown, though wrought in ancient days;
Tells of a few stout hearts, that fought and died,
Where duty plac'd them, at their country's side;
The man that is not mov'd with what he reads,
That takes not fire at their heroic deeds,
Unworthy of the blessings of the brave,
Is base in kind, and born to be a slave." —*Cowper.*

"My heart is always with my people."

—The Narragansett, in "The Wept of Wish-Ton-Wish."

Boy Soldiers of the Confederacy was covered in dust when found on an old bookshelf. Many years had evidently passed since its last reading. Opening the book revealed the old Confederate bill on this page, probably used as a book marker. Obviously, the bill reveals the wear of time, being torn and tattered, and is symbolic of the remaining thread for the call of Southern Independence.

FOREWORD

The moral fiber which bound the South together was very deeply entrenched within the boy soldiers. Account after account reveals the distinguishing acts of grandeur performed on the battlefield by the so called "Boy Soldiers." These acts of heroism were not planned acts of warfare but simply spontaneous reactions to the call of duty. Boys have impulsive reactions in contrast to the planned actions of mature men. Without those spontaneous acts, many of the skirmishes, battles and engagements would probably have been lost to the Union. Many incidents revealed the disciplined nature of these young boys when their ranks were broken by enemy fire. Ranks were closed to fill the void of their fallen comrade and the advancement proceeded. These young men never faltered during fire, but upon some occasions marched backwards while firing at the enemy and seeking a greater military position. Youth simply reacted to the call of their mother, the Southland. The Southland needed all of her sons to defend the Southern way of life. Northern aggression from Radical Republicans, malcontents, mercenaries and marauders forced the youth to defend their way of life. Multitudes of Europeans and other immigrants migrated to the aid of the Union in promise of new found wealth and individual recognition. No northern homes were being burned, farms destroyed, pillaged, financial wealth stolen or their female population exploited. Mothers and sisters of the boy youth of the South were insulted, raped and desecrated by those northern aggressors.

When a tyrannical government forms and subverts the human rights of its citizens, then it is the right of the people to defend their honor, integrity and personal wealth. These Southern Boy Soldiers simply wanted to maintain their traditions and live in peace. The peace was not to be, since on several occasions the South had called for a cessation of hostilities but the Northern Radicals remained unbent. Upon the battlefield, boy soldiers were treated the same as older soldiers when they presented themselves before the foe. Most every account of the youth utilized against the enemy were as a last resort or simply caught up in the heat of warfare. "War is hell" when the youth are caused to suffer from the sins of previous generations.

Most accounts of boy soldiers always indicated an undying devotion to their mother, country and God. The youth usually were greatly concerned about making their peace with God. After assuring themselves of their hereafter, they were willing to meet their destiny as Confederate Men. Many young boys fell on the battlefield of honor as did the cadets of Virginia Military Institute at the Battle of New Market. Several accounts illustrated the youthful smile on the boy soldiers as they lay mangled upon the hallowed ground. War will always be devastating to all, but accounts of atrocities toward the Southland and young Boy Soldiers should never be forgotten. The carnage of youth was very great. Many young southern soldiers were incarcerated with adult men in the Northern prisons. Without doubt the Union made decisions based solely upon bringing the Southland into submission.

Mrs. Susan R. Hull collated the information on the youth who helped to sustain the effort of the late Great Confederate States of America. Her endeavors were without doubt attributed to her brother Lieutenant Colonel John Baker Thompson of the First Arkansas, CSA. Colonel Thompson was the president of Saint Johns College in Little Rock, Arkansas, before the War for Southern Independence. He did not agree with secession but chose to honor the common threads that bound the southern way of life. This band of youth from Saint Johns College and Colonel Thompson entered into the service of the Confederacy. Saint Johns College was an institution begun by the Ancient Free and Accepted Masons of Arkansas. Masonry edicts, concepts, morals, ethics and caring for human kind were engraved upon the moral fiber of all the young boys who were under the leadership of Colonel Thompson.

The following individuals are recognized for their

assistance in this endeavor. My wife Jenni Ann Moore, (née Foster) assisted in the indexing phase. My Compatriot Mr. Jeffrey Ward Lloyd contributed his consul and helpful thoughts of the old State of Virginia.

The Southland was defeated by Union acts of attrition. It is heart-breaking to read accounts of Southern Soldier deaths but even greater when Boy Soldiers have given the supreme sacrifice. Without those acts of service to country and the homeland by previous generations, we as Americans would not enjoy the privileges and lifestyles of today.

It is through organizations such as the Sons of Confederate Veterans that we commemorate the lives and reverence those sacrifices by our fallen BOY SOLDIER HEROES. Our late great General Stephen Dill Lee gave the charge for all future generations to preserve the true history of the Southern Cause. BOY SOLDIERS of the CONFEDERACY is exemplary in illustrating the dedication by which the Southern Cause was born, fought and defeated. The Cause for which it stood is personified in the lives of those soldiers who served the Confederacy.

David J. Moore, Lieutenant Commander
P.O. Box 166
Grimes County Greys, Camp #924
Anderson, Texas 77830

The charge of the infamous Stephen Dill Lee, General CSA states:

"To you, Sons of Confederate veterans, we submit vindication of the cause for which we fought; to your strength will be given the defense of the Confederate soldier's good name, the guardianship of his history, the emulation of his virtues, the perpetuation of those principles he loved and which made him glorious, and which you also cherish. Remember it is your duty to see that the true history of the South is presented to future generations."

CONTENTS

CONTENTS—*Continued*

CONTENTS—*Continued*

CONTENTS—*Continued*

APPENDIX

APPENDIX I

APPENDIX II

APPENDIX III

ILLUSTRATIONS

BOY SOLDIERS OF THE CONFEDERACY

INTRODUCTION

In 1863 Gen. John E. Wool, then commanding in Baltimore, called and sent in his card with a request that I would see him immediately on important business. I found him walking up and down the floor in great agitation and apparently very angry, and Moore N. Falls, President of the Bay Line Steamship Company, trying in vain to pacify him. He said that the provost marshal—McPhail, I think—had ordered a draft of all boys of sixteen and over, and that he came to tell me that I might inform the Southern people, "for," he added, "what one of you knows, all know"; that he had revoked this order and would not permit it to be put in execution. He added, "This order once given, every boy in Maryland, all of whom are standing on tiptoe to cross the border, only held back by mothers and sisters, would be with Lee before night, and with an army of boys, Lee could whip the world. They are the best soldiers in the world, as they are incapable of fear because they do not know the meaning of danger." I declined the commission, as I naturally wished Lee to whip the world, and he posted his order himself. My attention being thus called to the boys, I noted all the facts that came under my observation, and kept all cuttings from newspapers, etc., bearing on the subject. I intended to admit to my roll of honor all boys under twenty, but I found so many were under sixteen—one of eleven, several of twelve, thirteen, etc.—that I will have to change the age of entrance to eighteen, save in exceptional cases. Even then I have to make the notices very short. When I first thought of making this collection, I only expected to show their bravery and reckless daring, but to my surprise I found that they were for the most part as remarkable for fervent piety as for the other qualities we naturally associate with boys. I shall give incidents of the boys just as I received them, careful to set down naught in malice nor aught in love extenuate.

ROBERT E. LEE, JR.

I place first in my record the name of Robert E. Lee, Jr., son of Gen. R. E. Lee, the stainless hero, the Christian gentleman of whom it has been said,

> "His life was gentle; and the elements
> So mixed in him that nature might stand up
> And say to all the world, *This was a man!*"

President Davis says while he was on duty in South Carolina and Georgia, Lee's youngest son Robert, then a mere boy, left school and came down to Richmond, announcing his purpose to go into the army. His older brother, Custis, was a member of my staff, and after a conference we agreed that it was useless to send the boy back to school, that he probably would not wait in Richmond for the re-

GENERAL LEE AND TRAVELER.

OPPOSITE PAGE 14.

turn of his father; so we selected a battery which had been organized in Richmond and sent Robert to join it. General Lee told me that at the Battle of Sharpsburg this battery suffered so much that it had to be withdrawn for repairs and some fresh horses, but as he had no troops even to offer a reserve, as soon as a battery could be made useful it was ordered forward. He said that as it passed him a boy, much stained with powder, mounted as a driver of one of the guns, said, "Are you going to put us in again, General?" After replying to him in the affirmative, he was struck by the voice of the boy, and asked him, "Whose son are you, my boy?" and was answered, "I am Robbie, father; don't you know me?" Whereupon his father said, "God bless you, my son, go on!"

Robert E. Lee, Jr., was afterwards on the staff of Gen. Fitz Hugh Lee. This is said to be the only instance on record where the son of a commanding general entered the army as a private in the ranks.

"A MERE BOY"

Dahlgren in his raid around Richmond was piloted by a negro, and when he reached the plank-road a few miles from the city he found it barricaded. Suspecting treachery or infuriated by defeat, he hung his wretched guide and left him on the tree. Making a detour to join Kilpatrick, who had already been routed by Maryland boys, he passed through King and Queen County, where he was ambuscaded—his men laden with plunder, silver, etc.,—captured, and he himself shot and instantly killed by "a mere boy." Papers found upon him showed from what a fate a bullet "shot at a venture" saved the city—sack, murder, rapine, negro uprising, fire. Though he was not first in command, Dahlgren was the inspirer of the plot and with his death it failed. He had already lost a leg at Hagerstown in an engagement with the same troops and officer that routed Kilpatrick.

EDMUND PENDLETON

Edmund Pendleton, of Fairfield, Clarke County, Va., joined the Army at seventeen, and displayed such gallantry that he was elected third lieutenant of his company. In the Maryland and Pennsylvania campaign of 1863 he was often put in command of select detachments to cover the retreat and make sudden dashes upon the enemy. In these skirmishes he would often capture as many prisoners as there were men in his command. At the severe engagement of Jenks Shops he led the brigade sharp-shooters. During the course of this battle his ammunition gave out and he resorted to the novel expedient of ordering his men to use stones, which were plentiful in this field. Himself starting the example, his men quickly obeyed and they succeeded in the assault. When asked why he followed this plan he said no body of men could have stood under the fire to which they were exposed without being engaged in some way. I have always thought it would be a good idea to raise a cairn to his honor at this point of the battlefield.

NOTE.—It has been suggested that with the powerful modern implements of war the romance of history would be lost, but the following incidents show that among the young soldiers of the present it still exists. I may be excused for remarking that one of these young officers is of Virginia and Maryland blood, the other of Maryland and New York ancestry.

After the battle of Guayama one of General Haines's staff officers said, "General, did you notice how your son got between you and the Spanish bullets?" The General replied that he had not, but that he *had* noticed he had been confoundedly in the way. When questioned, Lieutenant Haines admitted he *had* endeavored to shield his father, as he thought if anything happened he was better able to endure it, and his father's life was of more consequence than his.

Lieutenant Mervyn Buckey, of Maryland, had just graduated at West Point when the Spanish War broke out. He was put in command of a company, and when it landed on the shores of Cuba was told to wait until the other boats came with men and arms. As they stood on the shore unarmed, the Spaniards commenced firing from a house above them, and as Lieutenant Buckey's men dropped around him he realized that unless something was done they would become demoralized. So he ordered them to charge with stones, and unarmed they rushed upon the house and took it.

General Miles, from the boats, saw the whole affair, and as soon as he joined them promoted Lieutenant Buckey to the rank of captain, the only promotion made on the field during the Cuban war. He is only thirty years of age now, and is in command of the harbor of New York.

BARKSDALE WARWICK

Of Barksdale Warwick, of Richmond, aged sixteen, Gen. Henry A. Wise says: "As we drove the enemy the movement forward became slower and slower. I was pressing on the men with the words, 'Drive into them, boys; drive into them!' when Barksdale smiled and exclaimed, 'Let me cry charge, General Wise; let me cry charge!' 'Charge, my brave boy!' I replied, and he shouted 'Charge!' and bounded across the road and reached Lieutenant McDowell, and was shouting, 'Charge, charge!' with a bright smile on his face, when he was struck on the forehead and instantly killed. He did not seem to fall, but sat down on a log, and his head fell back against a tree, with its full expression of the '*gaudium certaminis*' on his face. After the surrender at Appomattox two officers of the Federal army, one a surgeon, told me he had been honorably buried and his grave marked. The surgeon said he had never seen so beautiful a corpse; that the color and smile were still on his face and he was sitting as he was left as if in repose, and with hardly a stain of blood or earth upon his person. He had been with me from the beginning of the war and had never failed in duty to his country or obedience to me. He was gentle and amiable, indomitable in courage and pluck, and his bravery was as natural and unaffected as his death was beautiful. After what has happened we ought not to wish such spirits still alive to suffer humiliation of submission."

LIEUTENANT NIEMEYER

Lieutenant Niemeyer entered the Army at eighteen. On the fatal field of Gettysburg, July 3, 1863, he was conspicuously brave. Three times his brigade halted and was aligned under a galling fire. After the last "halt and dress," when the regiment began to advance, Lieutenant Niemeyer turned to a comrade and brother lieutenant, with a bright smile on his face, and said, "John, what a beautiful line!" A few minutes after he fell dead, pierced through the head by a bullet. His body was never recovered, but fills one of the many "unknown graves" that furrow the hillside at Gettysburg.

I shall insert here an incident and poem, as I have thought the "young Confederate soldier" might have been Lieutenant Niemeyer or one of his "boys."

GETTYSBURG

"In going over the field of Gettysburg shortly after the battle we discovered the body of a young Confederate soldier, who in dying had fallen into a crevasse on the hill so deep that his remains could never be removed. As we looked at him a ray of sunshine fell on his face and he seemed smiling as if in triumph. The following lines were suggested by the incident:

" 'Far down the chasm within the mountain side
A wounded soldier fell, but ere he died
Upon his shattered arm his head he lay,
Turned his dim eyes toward the closing day
Gilding his brow as with celestial ray.
O'er his young face a smile of triumph played,
"I'll keep this place my valor gained," it said;

"No Arctic blast, no heat of summer sun,
No prayer of love, no shout of victory won,
No taunt of scorn, no curses, loud nor deep,
Can rend my tomb, nor wake me from my sleep.
Forever lying here, my manes shall show
Where Southern soldier met a Northern foe.
My soul to God, my country 'tis for thee
My life is given with purest ecstasy.
Across the stream, to reach the other side
My spirit flies, there, where our hero died.
He stands with arms outstretched upon the shore.
Saying, 'Come, soldier, come, and rest forevermore.'
Nameless I die, and yet for me shall rise,
Tho' marking not the place my body lies,
A monument, whene'er a prayer is said
Or tear of deathless memory shed
Above the tomb where sleep the unknown dead." ' "

"UNKNOWN DEAD"

I once asked a surgeon of Price's army, Dr. Paul J. Carrington, of Halifax County, Va., if he had ever seen a man he had killed. He said, *"No man, only a boy."* He always went into the fight, until the wounded began to be brought back, and, said he, often wondered whether the wounds he was trying to heal were those he had made. At the Battle of Pea Ridge a United States regiment wavered and began to run. A soldier stepped from the ranks, seized the colors, and waving them, tried to rally the men. His right arm was shattered and he took the flag in his left hand, still coming forward and urging the men to come on. He was shot and fell dead on the field. After the battle was over, Dr. Carrington, who had carefully noted the spot, went to see what manner of man it was had died so bravely. He found a boy, not over sixteen, the flag so tightly clasped in his hand that it would have taken force to disengage it. The facts were stated to the officer in charge of the burial party, and by his order the brave boy was laid to rest with the colors for which he had died wrapped around him. His name was not known, and he can only be remembered as one of the tenderly loved, "the unknown dead." It is less sad to think of him than of the loss of *my* unrecorded heroes. Though he fell, the cause for which he gave his life triumphed; while the banner for which our loved ones died is now but the emblem of a "Lost Cause."

When I began this record it was intended to be of boys on both sides, but I found so many very young Confederates that I decided to write of them only, especially as I was informed that a work on these lines about young Northern soldiers had already been published. I had some records of Northern boys which I returned to the senders thereof. But this young soldier had no friends known to me, and seems so lonely and far away that he shall be numbered with his "comrades in hospital," and rest with those who lie undiscovered in the hidden places where they fell; "the unknown dead," guarded by the changeless stars of heaven, undisturbed by the requiem of the

"Murmuring blast which
Mourns and laments in its wanderings past."

JACQUELINE BEVERLY STANARD

Jacqueline Beverly Stanard, aged seventeen, was wounded fatally in the Battle of New Market, but lived a short time and sent messages to his mother, telling her, "I fell where I wished to fall, fighting for my country, and I did not fight in vain. I die with full confidence in my God. My loved ones must meet me in heaven." As he caught the shout of victory from our men his trembling soul breathed itself to rest in a fervent, "Thank God!"

JIMMY MOORE

Colonel Pate, of the Fifth Virginia Cavalry, was killed in battle on the mountain road near Richmond. Little Jimmy Moore, his orderly, only sixteen years old, rode in under a storm of bullets and brought the body out. With the assistance of another man he took it into Dr. Shepherd's house, and had only time to pin a piece of paper with his name upon it to the breast when the enemy charged into the yard.

His exploit reminds one of the following: "Aaron Burr, when not more than sixteen, carried messages between Arnold and Montgomery through the thick of the fight at Quebec, and when Montgomery fell little Burr caught his body and carried it out of the line of fire through a very rain of bullets."

LESLIE CHAMBLISS DOVE

Leslie Chambliss Dove was born in Richmond, Va., December 24, 1845. He attended the best schools and a military academy under Col. Jasper Phillips. He won many prizes and was always devoted to study, particularly of the Revolutionary heroes, and committed many of their speeches to memory and laid them to heart. When South Carolina seceded he organized with his young companions a company which drilled daily, and when General Lee came to Richmond they offered their services. General Lee complimented their proficiency and skill, and admired their spirit, but said they were too young to serve. He then went to the Virginia Military Institute to prepare himself. But the war broke out, and he could not be satisfied to remain after hostilities began. The thought seemed to haunt him continually and he said he would consider himself eternally disgraced if he did not strike a blow in defense of his country. He determined to join the Army. Friends and relations urged upon him that he was too young to endure the duties and hardships of service. He said, "It is my duty to go where they are fighting, and if I can strike but one blow for the South, I mean to strike *that* blow." When told that his father would not consent to his entering the Army, he said, "Did Pa say so? Well, I have never disobeyed him before, but—I am going." His father gave a reluctant consent and he joined the Army. He served as a volunteer with a howitzer company from Richmond, in which command he had many friends. His health, never very robust, became seriously impaired, and he returned home after a campaign of several months. But on July 1st, 1863, he again set out to join the Army. His friend and cousin, General Chambliss, promising him a place on his staff, he was assigned temporarily to the duties of a courier—the Army was now in retreat from Gettysburg—and he served two days in this capacity, but near Front Royal was struck by a shell and mortally wounded. He was taken to the hospital and his friend, Dr. William Gregory, told him he could not survive the night. He said, "I expected it. Tell my father that I was not afraid to die." Though the army now moved on, kind friends saw to his burial and marked his grave, and after the war his remains were removed to Hollywood, where under a monument, a small model of the one to the Confederate soldiers, he rests, a noble type of the young Confederate soldier, and leaves to us only the solace of an honored grave. His frightened horse, riderless, rushed into the Federal line and was captured by an officer, who rode him into Richmond after the surrender. His father recognized it, and went to the officer and proved its history, and offered any price for it, but was refused.

HOWELL CHASTAIN EDMONDSON

Howell Chastain Edmondson, of Halifax County, Va., entered the army at sixteen. He was remarkable for cool, calm bravery. In one of the battles around Richmond, while the enemy was making a final assault, a comrade turned to Howell and asked him how he felt. Although under fire at the time, he calmly replied, "I fear no evil whatever, for I have long since made my peace with God."

WESLEY GRIGG

Wesley Grigg, of Petersburg, Va., entered the army at fifteen, under Captain Taylor Martin. He was made sergeant of one of the guns, which position he held with distinguished courage and efficiency in the ensuing campaign, till he surrendered with Lee at Appomattox. As an example of courage and heroism we give the following instance: "While the battery was stationed at Blandford Cemetery we were daily engaged in artillery duels with the enemy, in which candor compels me to state that Hotchkiss guns proved more effective than the iron Napoleons with which we were supplied. About half way between the lines was a tree which was a source of annoyance to Sergeant Grigg. As it was in line of his gun, the captain offered inducements to any of the company who would cut down the tree, with no effect, as it seemed certain death to attempt it. At length Sergeant Grigg stepped up and offered to cut it down, *if he was ordered to do so.* Taking an axe he soon reached the tree, and keeping time with his sturdy strokes to the solemn music of the whistling Minie, and an occasional shot or shell, he calmly cut till the tree was down, thinking all the time, as he afterwards said to me, 'that the only thing a soldier should do was to obey.' "

This illustration, selected from others, is sufficient to show the character of the youthful soldier. Not rash, but resolute in the discharge of duty. Not ambitious to reap honors for gallantry by voluntary exposure to danger, but ready to sacrifice his life at the command of a superior in whose judgment he had confidence, and at whose command it was his duty and pleasure to bow. Not zealous to reap applause from an heroic action, which appalled the hearts of older men, but ready to risk all when older men declined the sacrifice; and only then, when the captain would take the responsibility of what his friends might esteem rashness, and order him to do what he regarded a necessary thing for the safety and efficiency of his men. But as we learn from this same comrade (quoted above), when kindness and self-sacrifice were called for, Sergeant Grigg was ready always to render it, and when there was no hope of a reward. Thus he relates how one night, when he himself had fallen asleep on guard, from sheer exhaustion, under the fatigue of the previous day, on rousing up at roll-call, he was amazed and gratified to find Sergeant Grigg quietly walking his post for him.

CHARLES T. HAIGH

Charles T. Haigh was from Fayetteville, N. C. In his fifteenth year he saw his first active service with General Jackson. In 1863 he begged his father's permission to resign his cadetship, for though exempt by law, he thought it the duty of every one who could bear arms to go to the front. When the news of the Battle of Gettysburg reached him he said, "Boys, we must all join the Army; our country needs us; for my part, I can stay no longer here." He resigned and volunteered as a private in a North Carolina regiment. His first battle was in the Wilderness, where he acted with the coolness of a veteran. At Spottsylvania Court House his brigade was ordered to charge with others, a battery of the enemy, and it was there in that terrible horseshoe angle that Lieutenant Haigh lost his life for "Cause and Country." "Just as we emerged from the woods and dashed upon the guns he raised his arm, shouting, 'Charge, boys, charge! the battery is ours!" All the while the grape, canister, shrapnel, shell and round-shot were crashing through the trees and cutting down our comrades." And thus he died with the cry of victory on his lips, on the very ramparts of his country.

JOSEPH W. LATIMER

"Joseph W. Latimer entered the army at seventeen. He was very small, well formed, and of extremely youthful appearance. While on drill we paid him the utmost respect, and off drill we fondled and caressed him as if he were a child. He was the officers' pet, and we always called him 'our little Latimer.' One night after a tremendous battle, as we lay together on the ground, my little comrade drew closer to me and said, 'Well, Captain, I feel so thankful I have passed through this fight as well as I have.' Thinking he alluded to not having received a wound, I said I was more than glad he had escaped unhurt. He said: 'Oh! no. I do not mean that; I rather wish I had received a small wound so I might see how I bear it. What I meant was this—I was so glad I was able to stay at my post and do my duty in the fight. I have always felt a little afraid that I might lose my self-control and disgrace myself. I have tried it now, and have no anxiety for the future. He was afterwards promoted (a major at nineteen) and assigned to duty with Andrews's battalion, in command of which he received his fatal wound at Gettysburg. While gallantly cheering his men a fragment of shell struck his arm, shattering it completely. As he was carried off the field he passed his battery, and holding up the stump of his mangled arm, in a clear and steady voice exhorted them to fight harder than ever and avenge his loss. When he was taken from under his horse, which was killed when he lost his arm, he continued to give orders and seemed to think only of his command."

WILLIAM H. CABELL

William H. Cabell was only fifteen when the war broke out, and earnestly desired to join the volunteers, of which his brother, James Caskie Cabell, was lieutenant, but his father told him that having one son in the army, only seventeen, he was unwilling that another of tenderer years should become a soldier; so he reluctantly continued his studies at the Virginia Military Institute, where he graduated with the highest distinction. The theme and burden of his letters to his family was his longing to join the army of the South, saying repeatedly that he had rather die than that the contest should be over and independence achieved or lost without his contributing his mite to the struggle. In May, General Breckinridge called for the aid of the cadets to repel the Federal army under General Sigel, and though Cadet Cabell was very ill, he resolved to do his duty and undertook the march. It is said that he nearly fainted with debility, fatigued and overpowered by the labors of the way. At night, before the Battle of New Market, he spoke confidentially to a friend and fellow-student of the dangers of the impending conflict, saying that he feared nothing for himself, and that he was willing to incur the hazard, but of his brother, Cadet R. G. Cabell, who was not more than *sixteen*, he spoke in the tenderest terms. He feared that he would be either wounded or killed and deplored either event, as he knew it would cause the death of his broken-hearted mother. He retired a short distance from his comrades, and offered a prayer for his brother and himself, asking for protection in the expected battle, and then weary and worn, retired to his soldier's bed. On the 15th of May the Battle of New Market occurred, one of the most exciting of the war. The charges, rapid movement, impetuous action and the utter rout of the Northern forces, seldom occurred on one field. The Cadets rushed with all the enthusiasm and valor of youth to the charge, and every obstacle yielded to their unflinching and unfaltering courage. The Cadets were gloriously victorious. Cadet R. G. Cabell passed bravely and uninjured, and reached the enemy's cannon, while his noble, accomplished, beloved, and unfortunate brother was struck and torn by a fragment of a shell and lay mortally wounded in the path of the charge. It seems strange as well as terrible to think of one mother having *three* sons in an army under twenty-one years of age!

UNKNOWN DEAD

One boy whose name I have lost was wounded in one of the first battles of the war, in West Virginia. When his regiment was driven back, he stubbornly held his post. When the field was searched for the wounded he was still living, and said in broken whispers to a comrade who found him, "Tell mother,—died at post—remember, Casabianca." Captain R., who knew him, told me that he had insisted on enlisting, though he had two brothers in the army and was very young. Finding remonstrance in vain, his mother said, "My son, you can go, but you must first be prepared." He said, "I am prepared, I have my father's gun." She replied, "The Government will give you arms. I mean mental preparation. You are not going on a hunt, to return when you are tired; but if you go, it must be to stay and do your part. If you will read this life and learn these verses, and feel that you can do your duty like this boy, you may go." It was Casabianca. He went and manfully held his place. His officer is dead and I do not know if his mother ever received the message. His comrades said that he often told the story and repeated the verses by the camp fire.

W. U. MURKLAND

The students of Hampden Sidney College went in the army *en masse,* led by their professors. They were captured and paroled by General McClellan, who told them to return to college and attend to their studies. They accepted the parole "till exchanged." The Rev. Dr. W. U. Murkland, of the First Presbyterian Church, Baltimore, who was at the time not sixteen, was one of the number. It was a curious coincidence that when the McClellan family came to Baltimore to live they took a pew in Dr. Murkland's church and Dr. Murkland was one of the clergymen who officiated at General McClellan's funeral, sitting in the carriage with an officer who had been on General McClellan's staff when the students were captured.

JAMES BUCHANAN MURPHY

At the time of General Sheridan's march through the Valley of Virginia there was a call for volunteers to repel the invasion, and among others, James Buchanan Murphy, of Woodstock, not seventeen years of age, joined the army. After having had five horses shot under him, there was a desperate encounter, where a mere handful of Southern soldiers was opposed to the whole of Sheridan's army. A mistaken order to charge was given, and the hopelessness of it was so terrible that only *two* soldiers obeyed the fatal command, young Murphy and another, whose name is not known. Young Murphy was shot through the heart and his horse killed, his companion escaping as by a miracle. It reminds one of the Charge of the Light Brigade, only here there were but *two* instead of six hundred. One peculiarity I have noticed in the accounts of many of these boys—they died with a smile on their lips, that irradiated their faces when cold in death; also, that many of them, whom we might have thought were carried away by the recklessness and enthusiasm of youthful excitement, were boys of sincere conviction of the justice of their cause, true patriotism and consistent piety.

RANDOLPH

Colonel Smith, of the Virginia Military Institute, wrote me a letter, which I have mislaid, stating that a boy named Randolph, aged fourteen, enlisted in the cavalry, and reported to General Stonewall Jackson, as courier. During a battle he was sent with orders which were executed successfully; he returned, himself and his horse covered with blood. After keeping him through that campaign, General Jackson sent him to the Virginia Military Institute, and he was in the Battle of New Market. At the close of the war he became a clergyman. He is a cousin of General R. E. Lee, and a nephew of Bishop Randolph, of Virginia.

JOHN M'CUE

John McCue, of Staunton, Va., was at the Virginia Military Institute, and before he was sixteen

JOHN M'CUE.

OPOOSITE PAGE 32.

ran away and joined the cavalry in the Valley. He was captured on the Maryland side, while scouting with a number of his comrades, by a party of mounted police in United States uniform. They were hunting for horse thieves in the debatable land between the two armies, who, with deserters and run-away negroes, ravaged that unprotected country. In the mêlée one of his captors was killed, and young McCue was brought to Baltimore, to be tried for murder by court martial. His companions escaped. I received a note from his father, who was prisoner of war at Fort Delaware, asking me to do something for his son. I went to Captain Wigel, provost at the time, and asked him where the boy was. He said he was in jail, where he had been for some time, and that his case was hopeless, he would "certainly be hung," his trial beginning the next day. I asked him if I might have counsel for him. He said yes, but advised me not to "employ any Secesh lawyer," as it would prejudice the court martial against McCue. He gave me the name of a great Republican criminal lawyer, whom he advised me to employ; also one less distinguished, who would act as assistant for the other. On my way to engage the former, I met Mr. Frederick Brune, who offered to defend the boy (without payment, and never considering the risk to himself), though he considered Captain Wigel's advice good. I declined his kind offer. The Republican lawyer refused to take the case without a retainer of two hundred and fifty dollars (see note), an assistant and a note for the rest of one thousand dollars, given by his father, to be paid after the war. This lawyer, as far as I can remember, did not appear at all in the case, until the last day, and the assistant was worse than useless. The judge advocate was apparently deaf, and though he appeared willing to act fairly, could understand neither the boy nor myself. I was allowed to stay with him, to send for witnesses, in short to do anything that would give a legal color to an illegal trial.

The facts, as stated by McCue, were that being short of supplies, and believing the Marylanders to be favorable to them, they had crossed the Potomac, to get something to eat, not caring whether they had a little brush with the enemy or not. When the police attacked them they resisted, as they thought they were United States soldiers, and that, though he would have shot if he could, as an actual fact his opponent had him down, when his pistol went off in the struggle. The man that was killed was twice the size and strength of the boy. I interposed here with a question as to whether the course of the ball would not confirm this, stating that I believed him, for McCue came of a truthful, upright, and honorable family, that claimed that no member of it had ever been before a court for crime, or told a falsehood. This, however, could not be determined, as the body had been buried without special examination. I was asked if I had any witnesses, and I had none, as the boy positively refused to name his comrades, even if they could have been reached. I summoned, however, his father, then a prisoner of war at Fort Delaware, and his mother, then in Staunton, Va. They knew nothing of the affair, but I thought it was the last opportunity for them—to bid adieu to their boy. The mother could not come. The father came with a guard. Imagination can scarcely conceive his feelings when he saw his son in that dreadful position, he powerless to save him. When asked if he knew the prisoner, he said, "He is my son, sir." Even those stern men were affected. McCue was perfectly calm when brought into court in his sad, ragged cadet uniform. His only anxiety was lest his appearance should betray the straits of his people. He begged that he might be suitably dressed, but we explained to him that it was advisable for him to wear the gray. Before the court he answered freely any questions about himself; any that would implicate his companions, he declined to answer. Asked where he crossed, he refused to say; the names of his companions, he declined to tell. "Did you receive the aid you expected?" "No."

The last day of the trial came. The $1,000 lawyer came with a speech, purporting to be the plea of the prisoner, begging for mercy on the ground that he was a conscript and forced into the army. The boy utterly repudiated it. He jumped to his feet and said: "I was *not* conscripted. I ran away from school to join the army. I would rather they took me out and shot me now, than have it go back to my people that I said I was a conscript." Remember in what circumstances he was placed, a mere boy without a friend within reach but me, whom he had not seen since he was a child, with the dread panoply of a court martial before him, expecting a speedy, ignominious death; yet calm, undaunted, he displayed a fortitude unequalled. It is comparatively easy in the crash of battle to forget death, but coolly to look it in the face in a situation like this required far more courage. He was condemned to imprisonment at hard labor for life, in the Fitchburg Penitentiary, but was pardoned by General Grant, at the intercession of his mother, and upon the information given by one of the members of the court martial, Colonel Bowman, I believe, that the verdict was a compromise offered by him to save the boy's life. It is noble acts like this, and his conduct at Appomattox, that endear the memory of General Grant to the Southern heart, and I hope some day there will be raised at Arlington a monument to the two heroes, Lee and Grant, similar to that erected to Wolfe and Montcalm on the heights of Abraham, showing to all time a united people combining to honor two heroes, who, each faithful to his own conviction of duty, fought bravely till the war was ended and laid down his arms, the one conquered the other conqueror, alike without a stain upon their honor, one bitter thought in the breast of the conquered, or one of malicious triumph in that of the conqueror.

NOTE.—This account was written immediately after McCue's release. His picture, which I have just received, was taken some time after he had left prison, and shows what a mere child he was when convicted, as does the pen picture in a letter, also just received, from Judge Dorsey, of Oakland Mills, Howard County, Md., of how he appeared when he enlisted. "I was with Colonel Mosby when he reached the command, a slight, beardless boy in his V. M. I. uniform, mounted on the smallest pony I ever saw in my life, with no other arms than a pistol of the smallest caliber. He pulled this pistol out and said what he would do with the Yankees when he met them. My brother said, 'McCue, if you were to shoot me with that pistol I would think a mosquito bit me.' However, in the first engagement Johnnie led the way when the charge was ordered, and captured a big Yankee, ordering him to surrender with his little pistol in his face. Johnnie got the man, horse and equipment, and came out a hero, and the most enthusiastic boy you ever saw. [I think it was probably this equipment that tempted him to forage in Maryland.—S. R. H.] He was very slight in figure, but had a lion heart." He had no idea that he might be hung, and asked me, when he thought things looked black for him, "Please ask them, when they shoot, not to hit my face. I've grown so much since mother saw me, she would not know me unless she saw that." The lawyer did not receive the balance of the $1,000, as the father lost his all in the war—and it was *just,* for one word from him would have shown the illegality of the trial. John should have been treated as a prisoner of war. He was simply a soldier foraging in the enemy's country. Perhaps it was natural that the lawyer, who spent most of his time in Washington, should think affairs of the nation of more importance than the life of a poor little rebel boy.

A BRAVE BOY'S ANSWER

Among the prisoners brought from West Virginia to Baltimore was Captain Henry Robinson, of Staunton, who told me of the following incident: There were many boys captured with him. They were hungry, tired, some barefooted, all ragged; some bareheaded or with the merest apologies for hats. As they passed down Madison Street, near Charles, on the way to jail, Miss M—— G——, who was looking at them, exclaimed sneeringly, "Is *this* your Southern *chilvary?*" One young fellow threw off his brimless hat, and turning to her said, "Yes, madam, yours to command for service; save these bonds!"—pointing to the guards. Miss G. then exclaimed, "They've actually read the Bible!" Both guards and prisoners gave a rousing cheer and Miss G. retired. Captain Robinson told me he could not understand how boys that had never been in battle stood so well or bore the fatigues of march and deprivation with such patience, even gaiety.

LITTLE JIMMY

Mrs. Thorburn, wife of Commodore Thorburn, while visiting the hospital at Greensboro, N. C., saw a boy, a mere child, about thirteen. She asked him his name and how he came there; but he was so much afraid he would not be allowed to go back into the army that he would only say his name was "Jimmy," and that he had broken his arm in the fall of the platform as he got off the cars at Greensboro. Mrs. Thorburn became much interested in him, and told her daughter, a child of eleven, to go in and talk to Jimmy, and perhaps she could persuade him to tell something of his family. After several visits from her, he began to talk of himself; said he had neither father nor mother, only a little sister, whom he loved dearly; that he lived in Mississippi, near Vicksburg, and knowing an officer in command some distance from home, he had run off to enlist, to fight for his country. He had expected to be received with joy, but the officer told him he was too young and must return, giving him money and a pass. When he reached Greensboro he got off to get some food, and the crowd was so great the platform gave way and he was hurt. He bore his wounds with fortitude, looking forward to the time when he could again make the attempt to join the army. It was found necessary to amputate his arm, and he said he could stand it if the little girl who "reminds me of my sister" would stay with him. This she did, and as chloroform was administered to the patient, doubtless suffered more than he—an act of heroism on her part as great as any shown during the war. In fact, her many noble deeds would have been worthy of a far older person. The arm seemed to be doing well. One day, when Mrs. Thorburn went to see Jimmy, he said, "I see a bright light around me." "No, Jimmy," she said, "it is rather a dark day." "But," he said, "I am in a bright shining light. Let me put my arms around you, and—kiss me once, Mrs. Thorburn, I feel so lonely." She said, "Certainly, my darling child, kiss me as often as you like." She put her arms around him and he rested his head on her shoulder. She said, "Let's say that little prayer you love so much." He closed his eyes as he said the prayer, and folded his hands upon his breast and she laid him on his pillow, thinking he was asleep. He was—sleeping the sleep that knows no waking, till his eyes are opened in brighter climes than this poor world of ours. Like St. Stephen, he saw the heavens opened and a shining pathway from earth to heaven upon which his innocent soul was wafted to eternal glory.

Bertie Thorburn, the little girl here mentioned, was most beautiful, with mind and heart far in advance of her years. It is an interesting coincidence that at the time she was acting her part in the great tragedy, in North Carolina, her future husband, a cadet of twelve, was taking notes in Richmond, which have just been published, and which I consider the most interesting personal narrative I have seen since the war.

WILLIAM PEYTON ESKRIDGE

This was no isolated case. All the boys in the South, however young, interested themselves in the war. William Peyton Eskridge, son of William and Mary Randolph Eskridge, of Staunton, Va., being entirely too young to be of service in the field, did all he could to help the ill and wounded, prisoners and Confederates. He obtained books for them from relatives and friends after exhausting those of his family, and I have many volumes scribbled over with names and remarks of soldiers who read them then. It was very difficult to procure necessary food,—and luxuries, almost impossible,—and the little fellow foraged in every direction and carried his spoils to the hospital, and many fever-parched lips welcomed the cooling fruit he triumphantly displayed.

DAVIS

If the only son of President Davis had reached the age of boyhood I should have placed his name first in my records. He was a very delicate child, and died in his beautiful home at Richmond, now appropriately the Museum for Relics of the Confederacy. His playmates erected a beautiful monument to him in Hollywood, where he rests with the young soldiers of the South, some of them his companions in mimic warfare, who, afterwards entering the army, lost their young lives and joined him on the other side.

UNKNOWN DEAD

A surgeon in Baltimore told me that three boys captured while foraging were brought to the hospital, all (as supposed) slightly wounded. They were so young, ragged, dirty, grimed with blood and mud that he thought they were only some young roughs who had been caught in mischief. He examined them and found all but one had trivial scratches, but the third was a hopeless case, bleeding to death internally. He ordered him to remain, and said the others could be carried on. The boy, after looking at him for a moment, said, "Am I as bad as that?" The surgeon said, "Yes, my boy, I am afraid you are." He was silent a moment, and then said, *"Dulce et decorum est pro patria mori."* Said the surgeon, "My boy, where did you learn that?" He replied, "We have just left school, sir." He then turned to one of his companions and began, "Tell mother—" The surgeon was called off to a desperate case and did not return until his companions had gone and he was resting, covered with a sheet, his hands folded, a smile on his face as if in childhood's sleep. I heard of a similar case from a gentleman who visited the field hospitals at Gettysburg. He said: "I was astonished at the expression on many of the faces of the Rebel dead. They so often seemed smiling triumphantly, though dying defeated. One wounded boy struck me particularly. I was going over the field to help take off the wounded and found a boy who was shot in the breast. He seemed a mere child and I said, 'What are you doing here?' He said, 'Where else, sir?' I said, 'At home with your mother.' He laid his hand over the bleeding wound, and looking me calmly in the eye, said, 'For home and mother.' We took him to the tent and he made no moan, though the wound, which was slight, must have been very painful. I think he will recover. It made me really sick," he added.

BENNETT H. YOUNG, THE MAN WHO BEARDED MORGAN

Bennett H. Young, the Kentucky lawyer who upset all precedent by treating J. Pierpont Morgan as an ordinary witness when he testified in the Louisville and Nashville deal in the Federal building, proved a surprise to the wealth of New York legal talent, who have made it a rule to deal with the great financier with kid gloves. Mr. Morgan did not know what to make of Mr. Young. Neither did the other lawyers. The tall, suave, white-haired Kentuckian, with imperturbable politeness but with an insistence that knew no limit, kept Mr. Morgan on the rack for a full hour and drew from him information which he probably never dreamed of giving. But to the few who knew the Kentuckian, his refusal to be overawed by Mr. Morgan, or anybody

BENNETT H. YOUNG.

OPPOSITE PAGE 42.

else, was not surprising. Mr. Young, in addition to being a railroad lawyer, is a genuine Kentucky colonel—a fighter from the ground up, when fighting is necessary, but in the ordinary affairs of life a quiet, soft-voiced courteous man of the world. Colonel Young's fighting record was established in the Civil War. Had Mr. Morgan known of one feat of reckless daring performed by him back in 1864 he would have better understood the caliber of the man pitted against him.

Colonel Young, aged twenty-one, was the man who, on October 19, 1864, led a band of Confederates into the town of St. Albans, Vt., and gave the residents of that place a practical example of what the residents of scores of Southern towns had suffered. The St. Albans raid, as it is called, fills a unique place in the history of the Civil War. Nobody ever dreamed of a band of armed Southerners invading a town in Vermont. That section of the country, so far removed from the actual scene of strife, was supposed to be absolutely safe. Colonel Young at that time was a lieutenant in the Confederate Army. He had served with that other Morgan, so well known in the South, the cavalry raider, and had learned the trick of making sudden onslaughts in unexpected places. To escape capture and imprisonment by the United States forces he had previously fled to Canada. In Toronto he met many exiled Southerners. Among these the plan to attack St. Albans was worked out, the prime purpose being to spread dismay, if possible, among the Union forces, for the safety of New England towns. It was proposed to secretly organize raids, cross the border from time to time, and serve the frontier towns as Sherman was treating the people of Georgia; but this was overruled as being impracticable. A few of the hot-heads, however, who were not convinced, secretly met and matured a little plan on their own hook, unknown to the majority, of which the following was the *finale*. They planned to raid the banks of the town and carry off what money could be found for the use of the Confederate cause. Lieutenant Young was chosen leader of the enterprise.

Like a clap of thunder in a clear sky, one morning the news flashed over the wires that "a Rebel horde" had captured St. Albans, Vt. Subsequent news revealed the fact that the "Rebel horde" consisted of twenty-six men under the command of Lieutenant Young, of Kentucky. By preconcerted action they arrived in St. Albans as ordinary passengers, and the weather being exceedingly cold, it was not strange that each should be enveloped in a long ulster. They met in the St. Albans Hotel, matured their plans, and at a given signal the next morning each one threw off his overcoat and stood revealed to the citizens a full-fledged Confederate soldier, armed *cap à pie*—that is, every man had a latest improved Colt's revolver in each hand. The leader demanded the instant and unconditional surrender of the city. The mayor and city officials, after a hurried consultation, acceded to the demand, and the entire male population was corralled in the public square.

A chain guard was placed round the prisoners, while four of the attacking party went through the banks and confiscated about $200,000 in greenbacks and Government bonds. Sergeant —— had a narrow escape. A citizen, more combative than the others, drew a bead upon him with a rifle, but was detected in time to seal his own doom. That was the only casualty that occurred. The Southerners lost no time in making their way across the border, and the Federal Government immediately demanded their extradition as marauders. They were arraigned before the police judge in Toronto, and they pleaded that they were belligerents, not robbers, being regularly enlisted as commissioned Confederate soldiers. The very best counsel was secured and a motion to grant a continuance for twenty days, in order that they might procure evidence, was granted. A messenger volunteered to go to Richmond, Va., for papers, but found such difficulty in getting through that the twenty days passed and he had not returned. The trial began; it could be no longer delayed. It was nearly over and every one thought the prisoners were lost; but just at the close the messenger arrived and in the most dramatic manner opened a travel-stained bag and unrolled several letters obtained in Richmond, showing that the prisoners were belligerents, within the meaning of the law; and they were discharged accordingly.

Secretary Seward brought vigorous measures to bear upon the Dominion Government, the newspapers of Canada set up a howl against the men whose conduct was calculated to plunge the country into a broil with the United States, and the upshot was that Parliament was convened in session extraordinary within a week; and an "alien and sedition" law, empowering the Governor-General to suspend the writ of *habeas corpus* in the case of aliens, and order them out of the Dominion within forty-eight hours, was railroaded through Parliament.

Inside forty-eight hours after the passage of the Bill, every Confederate prisoner was making tracks from Canada. Some took their chances to pass through the Federal lines; others drifted into the North and remained there, *incognito,* until the close of the war; while others crossed the water with a view to taking passage on a blockade runner and entering a Southern port. While waiting for a vessel to be fitted out at Glasgow, Lee surrendered, and each took his own course in getting home.

The St. Albans raid formed an important point subsequently in the Geneva arbitration, and Secretary Stanton declared it to be one of the most significant events of the war, as it threatened to involve Great Britain in the civil strife.

Colonel Young is one of the pillars of the Presbyterian Church in Louisville, but nobody ever fools with him. He has been known to do a few things successfully in the way of calling down swashbucklers and professional "bad men" that only a man with a big "gun" handy, and the nerve to use it quickly, would ever attempt. His father was a Presbyterian divine, and his first wife was a daughter of Rev. Dr. Stuart Robinson, a famous Presbyterian minister in Kentucky years ago. Colonel Young is quiet and modest, but he has four boasts which he sometimes makes. These are:

"I never swore an oath.

"I never told a lie.

"I never drank whiskey.

"I never touched a card."

And he might truthfully have added: "The man doesn't live that I am afraid of."

He is sixty-five years old. He is tall, spare and rawboned, but has the unmistakable set-up of the soldier. His hair, moustache and goatee are snow-white. The set of his jaws and a peculiar glint in his eyes are the only signs of the fighter. He is erect, broad-shouldered and physically alert. He knows railroading from A to Z and built the Louisville Southern Road, now part of the Southern Railroad system. People in its territory always speak of it as "Bennett Young's road." And the big, high bridge across the Kentucky River, which he built, they always call "Bennett Young's bridge."

The lack of detailed railroad knowledge displayed by Mr. Morgan on the stand surprised him. He said he would call Mr. Lanier, one of Mr. Morgan's fellow voting trustees in the Southern system. Francis Lynde Stetson, Mr. Morgan's lawyer, told Colonel Young that Mr. Lanier knew nothing about the questions involved of the details of the road.

"He doesn't know less about railroads than Mr. Morgan, surely," said the Colonel, in his softest tones, to Mr. Stetson.

Colonel Young's son, Lawrence Young, now president of the Washington Jockey Club in Chicago, was the most famous college baseball pitcher in the country. He pitched for Princeton four years, and had an almost unbroken record of victories.

Five years ago Colonel Young married for the second time. As soon as the hearing ended in the Federal Building, he said to the writer:

"I'm going to start right away for Louisville."

"What is your hurry, Colonel?"

"I'll tell you, my boy. I've got a little two-and-a-half-year-old baby at home. When I started for here she put her arms around my neck and said, 'Come home soon, papa.' I said I would, and I'm going to keep my word."

But before he left the room the courtly old gentleman who had caused Mr. Morgan so much worry went to everybody in the room—opposing lawyers, commissioners, witnesses, reporters, stenographers and court-room attaches—and shook each one ceremoniously by the hand.

If the reader will consider that St. Albans had, at that time, a population of about three thousand five hundred, that it had an able-bodied male population, fit for military service, of about seven hundred and fifty, that it was located in the heart of the most populous section of the country, honey-combed with railroad and telegraph lines, and that this "Rebel horde" (of twenty-six men, led by a boy) were many hundred miles from their base of supplies, he will agree that, for daring, it stands without a parallel among daring deeds.

HEROISM OF SAM DAVIS

"You doubtless have seen that the Legislature, by a resolution, has appropriated a spot upon the acropolis for a monument to this young man. And the questions might be asked: Why did the Legislature pass such a resolution? Who was Sam Davis? Did he lead listening Senates? Was he ever a governor of the State? Did he lead our legions to battle? What did he do, that the Legislature of this

State should have given to him a place by the side of James K. Polk and Andrew Jackson, two Presidents of the United States; one who slept for many years in sight of the Capitol, but whose tomb was allowed to be placed upon the Capitol site; and Andrew Jackson, a man national in his fame, a man glorious, a man known to all the earth; and out of all the Tennessee people since the Capitol was built, only these two have been allowed resting places there—one in his grave and the other astride of his bronze horse? Then who was Sam Davis? That is what the committee has asked me to tell.

"It is a simple story of a short life and a death so glorious that it has no rival. His father and mother came to the State of Tennessee from Virginia, that State that has furnished so much of good and so much of greatness to the world. I take it, as they came from Virginia and from his simple English name, that he came of English blood. He lived the life of other Tennessee boys, and was at a military school here by Nashville in 1861, when the cloudburst of war started the American people. Tennesseean-like, the young man, scarcely nineteen, volunteered in the first regiment he could reach, which was the First Tennessee Regiment, C. S. A.

"I have asked a soldier comrade of that regiment, who was afterwards connected with his family, about him, for I felt certain that you would desire to hear of a man so famous, of a man capable of so heroic a deed, that any particular would be interesting. Sam Davis was nearly six feet high, and was as straight and slender as a mountain pine. He had a shock of hair black as the raven's wing, and his face was bronzed, his eyes black and shining like diamonds. He was gentle and kindly as a girl. He loved his mother, and was gentle in his demeanor to his soldier comrades; while everybody who knew him was fond of him. He entered the Army and served some time with the First Tennessee, and then was selected to compose a company of scouts on the dangerous duty of invading the enemy's line. That service went on until in November, 1863, when he was captured by the Federal soldiery near the town of Pulaski, Tenn. There were found upon his person maps of fortifications of Nashville and other places, statistics of the Federal army, their numbers in infantry, their artillery, cavalry, and all it takes to make up an army.

"General Dodge, who was the commander of the Federal corps then at Pulaski, sent for him. He made known to the young man the grave and serious condition which he was in; that he would have to call a court martial to try him for a spy. General Dodge said to him: 'If you will give me the name of your informant; if you will tell me where these maps and figures came from, I will set you free.' General Dodge evidently supposed that they came from around his headquarters, either from a staff officer or somebody in the confidence of a staff officer; he was very pressing in his desire to get this information. He says himself: 'I was struck with admiration at the integrity, the dignity, and the splendid courage of this young man, and I did my best to save his life.'

"The court martial was called. Two charges were submitted. Charge first was that he was a spy. Charge second was that he was inside Federal lines carrying upon his person maps and communications detrimental to the government and to the armies of the United States. The specifications of both charges were set out.

"To the first charge and specification he pleaded not guilty. 'I am here in my Confederate uniform, without concealment. *I am not a spy.*' To the second charge he pleaded guilty. The court martial, after a long investigation, found him guilty upon both charges and specifications. And when that was done he was confined in a separate cell, and the fact was made known to him that he had to die.

"On November 26, 1863, on Thursday night, this young fellow, in his lonely cell, wrote a letter most pathetic to his mother and father. He said: 'I am going to die on the gallows tomorrow. Do not grieve for me; it will do no good. Think of me; do not forget me. Tell the children to be good. I am not afraid to die.'

"Next morning there was sent to the jail a wagon to take him to the place of execution, under the orders of the court martial. One of his comrades, who had been captured at the same time, but was confined with others as a prisoner in the court-house of the little town, said they heard the drum roll, they saw the regimental march, and sitting in the wagon they saw their comrade and their friend. When he saw them he arose to his feet and bowed. He was taken on, over to the eastern portion of the city, on a bluff-side, and there, sitting on a bench, he awaited the action of the military authorities.

"General Dodge, thinking that in the presence of the scaffold, in the presence of immediate death, this young hero might have changed his mind, and that he might give him the information that he so much desired, sent Captain Chickasaw, his chief scout, to him. He touched him on the shoulder with his hand, and said: 'It is not too late. Give me the information, and you will be escorted to the Confederate lines.' That scaffold loomed up, and was a hideous spectre in his front, but he turned and said: 'Captain, give my thanks to General Dodge for the interest he has taken in me; but if I had a thousand lives, I would surrender them here and now before I would do a thing like that; betray my friends or the name of my informer.'

"Look at the gracious and sweet demeanor—no bluffing, no bravado, no defiance, and no truculence—of that gallant young spirit on the verge of his grave! He was a gentleman. He had the gentleness in him to thank his enemies for the courtesies that they had done him. He asked Captain Armstrong: 'How long have I to live?' He replied: 'Fifteen minutes.' Davis said: 'The boys will have to fight the balance of the battles without me.' Captain Armstrong said: 'I hate to do this thing; I would rather die myself.'

"Standing around that scaffold were the stern phalanxes of the Government, under orders, with their guns in their hands. This young man was alone. He was twenty-one years and a few months of age. He had no counsel; he had no friend; he had no backer; that terrible thing was before him, and the resolution that he had was of his own making. He arose to his feet and looked around. What did he see? He looked upon the sun for the last time. Life is very, very sweet. It is particularly sweet when we are about to lose it. The sun that had kissed his cheek to a tan for twenty-one years was giving him her last kiss; the breeze that waved his raven hair was blowing on it for the last time; the hills of Pulaski were standing silent around him. Nearness to death must have quickened his faculties—and how he must have loved to live; how that heroic young spirit must have hated to die! Through his veins was running blood like quicksilver, singing to him the song of life. The earth was very beautiful; the sky was very blue. He could almost hear the dropping of the tears of his mother; he could hear her low moan and the groan of agony that came from his father. Perhaps there was another somewhere in Tennessee who was on her knees at that time—somebody must have loved that glorious young fellow. He could look over toward the South, and there he could see the hard-pressed flag of his country, and he could hear the shout of his comrades fighting for what they believed was just. Oh, how he must have hated to leave them to fight that battle alone—this gallant, glorious, and devoted young soldier! He died with the calmness of a philosopher, the sternness of a patriot, and the serene courage of a martyr. Never did a deeper gloom spread over any community than did over that of Pulaski when Davis's tragic fate was made known. The deed was openly and boldly stigmatized by the common soldiers as a needless assassination; men and women in every part of the town indulged in unavailing moans, and even the little children, with terror depicted on their countenances, ran about the streets weeping with uncontrollable grief. No man ever awakened a deeper sympathy. His sad fate is one of the touching themes of the country; and whenever his name is mentioned, the tear rises unbidden to the eye of the oldest as well as of the youngest. His memory is embalmed among the people as a self-immolated martyr to what he conceived a pure and holy duty—the preservation of the sacredness of confidence. This case furnished a melancholy example of the atrocities still permitted under the usages of civilized warfare."

The following is copy of a pass given scouts, such as Sam Davis carried when captured:

"Guards and Pickets Pass.................... through all our lines with or without countersign.

"BRAXTON BRAGG,
"General Commanding."

BROTHER AGAINST BROTHER

Nothing is more pathetic than the fratricidal nature of the Civil War—Brother against brother, father against son; relatives of the same name, brought together, not in family reunion, but in the fierce strife of battle. For example: Admiral Poor bombarding Norfolk, and his son defending the walls. Two young men from York, Pa., twin brothers, Milton and Horace Bonham, fighting in the ranks, one from Mississippi, one from Pennsylvania.

When Bonham, of Mississippi, went to see his brother in York, Pa., after the war there was great difficulty in preventing his being lynched for having gone South.

General Braxton Bragg, most ardent in his efforts to substitute the Confederate banner for the United States flag, and his namesake and relative having this record at Sumter: "In the death of Major Henry M.

Bragg, a brave and gallant young officer, whose fortune it was when a mere youth to participate in some of the most stirring scenes of our great rebellion, has passed from our midst in the prime and pride of early manhood. Major Bragg's active war service commenced in 1861, at the tender age of seventeen, as lieutenant in the Thirteenth Regiment of New York Militia, at that time serving in Virginia. In September, 1862, he was commissioned a lieutenant in the One Hundred and Thirty-ninth Regiment of New York Volunteers, was appointed a captain and aide-de-camp by President Lincoln in August, 1863, and in March, 1865, received the brevet of major, for 'gallantry and meritorious conduct' during the war. From August, 1862, until the close of the war, he served upon the staff of Major-General Gillmore as aide-de-camp, taking part in the campaign in central Kentucky during the autumn, winter, and spring of 1862-'63; in the operations against Charleston in 1863, comprising the assault of Morris Island, the reduction of Fort Sumter, and the siege and capture of Fort Wagner; and in 1864 in the battle of Drewry's Bluff, and all the numerous engagements of the Tenth Corps in the vicinity of Bermuda Hundred and Petersburg. In the winter and spring of 1865 he again served upon the coast of South Carolina, was present at the reoccupation of Charleston by the Union forces, and with his own hands replaced our flag upon the ramparts of Fort Sumter. Upon the reorganization of the Regular Army in 1866, he was appointed a lieutenant in the Second Regiment of Infantry, and in November of that year was, at his own request, transferred to the Third Regiment of Cavalry, serving with it in several campaigns against the Indians for a period of over three years, until forced to retire from the service by impaired health.

"In the subject of this brief sketch a physical organization of the most sensitive delicacy was conjoined to great force of character, high personal daring in the presence of danger, and conspicuous gallantry upon the field of battle. He was a gentle and most devoted son and brother, a generous and beloved comrade, and a brave soldier."

A singular instance of identity of names is in evidence in Baltimore now. Kirby Smith, Esq., one of the professors at the Johns Hopkins University, is a son of General Kirby Smith, of the U. S. Army, but a namesake of General Kirby Smith, of the Confederate Army. The two generals met in battle and the Union general was so struck by the conduct of his adversary that he named his first-born son in his honor. He wished it to be distinctly understood that his son was named for his adversary and not for himself. These men did not retain the bitterness of the fight—each found something to admire and respect in the other.

I am sure the Hon. R. M. T. Hunter, Secretary of the Confederate States, would have blushed to acknowledge his relative, General Hunter, U. S. A., of the Valley campaign.

Capt. I. M. E. Valk, of West Virginia, was captain and quartermaster of the Ninth North Carolina Regiment, and his brother, Dr. Wm. W. Valk, was member of Congress from New York and a surgeon in the United States Army.

It seems almost incredible that there was an Abraham Lincoln on both sides—the President, and another Abraham Lincoln, a private in the First Virginia Cavalry, Company F, Jefferson County. He deserted in 1864, so the other side may have him too.

Miss Meredith, of Baltimore, told me since the war that the greatest anguish she ever endured was in seeing her brother, Gilmor Meredith, an officer in the Fifth Maryland, arming to repel the Seventh New York, of which her nephew, Meredith Howland, was a member.

WASHINGTON COLLEGE, NOW WASHINGTON AND LEE UNIVERSITY

In reply to a toast, "Liberty Hall Volunteers, the student heroes of 1861, to whom Liberty and the honor of their country were more dear than life itself," Hon. Wm. A. Anderson, at the Alumni Dinner of Washington and Lee University, June 15th, 1892, spoke as follows:

In March, 1861, a secession flag was run up in the night above the statue of Washington, but the act was disapproved by the faculty and by the great body of students. At the request of the President of the College, that great and good Dr. George Judkins, the flag was taken down by Willie Preston, with the approval of his fellow students; that same Willie Preston who afterwards glorified the illustrious name he bore, by a heroic death, which he met at the Second Battle of Manassas, in the memorable charge of the Stonewall Brigade, under the leadership of that knightly Christian soldier, Hugh A.

White, captain of the Liberty Hall Volunteers. The question of secession was argued for and against by every body of men in the Southern States. Always conservative, Washington College saw in secession no remedy for any wrong; no security for any right. But, while devoted to the Constitution and willing to surrender every thing but honor and liberty to prevent the disruption of the Union, the men and youths who made Washington College what it then was, believed that their first allegiance was to their State, and that it was not in the constitutional power of the Federal Government to *coerce* a State. When war, unconstitutional war, was begun upon our sister States by the Government at Washington, Virginia, with a courage unsurpassed in history, took position with the weaker side, not *for dis-union,* but against *coercion.* At first call to arms a military company was formed by the students of the College. They were presented by the women of Falling Spring, Rockbridge County, with a flag, upon which was embroidered the coat of arms of Virginia, and the motto, "*Pro aris et focis.*" That banner was conspicuous afterwards upon the perilous edge of battle; its lovely folds were stained and rent and torn in the hailstorm of shot and shell through which it was borne by the young hands to which it was entrusted. Though thus rent and torn and stained, it was never trailed in dishonor! There was not a boy in that company who would not have laid down his life, his young life, cheerfully to shield that little banner from shame or ignominy. It was the flag of Virginia, the ensign of their Alma Mater. Before the country had realized that war was upon us, the company was accepted by the then Governor of Virginia, John

FRONT CAMPUS OF WASHINGTON AND LEE UNIVERSITY.

OPPOSITE PAGE 58.

Letcher. It was a beautiful spring morning the order was given to march. Behold them—a company, 64 strong, composed of slender youths; their average age, not seventeen or eighteen years; their average weight 130 pounds. There is an earnestness in them, a resolute expression on their youthful faces; there is a light of liberty, a glance of glory in their eyes, only seen when men, high in hope, are about to enter on some arduous enterprise of danger or duty. The tender farewells have been spoken and eyes have gazed into other eyes that will meet their loving glance no more. Mr. Wm. Dodd offered a prayer which seemed to have been inspired. Tears came into many eyes in those youthful ranks, but with smiles shining through their tears, with elastic step the already well-drilled volunteers marched away to the field of their glory. Soon afterwards they were assigned to the Fourth Virginia Infantry Brigade of General T. J. Jackson. From that day, when this company marched from Lexington to join the army, in every battle in which General Jackson was engaged, and after his untimely death in every battle in which the Army of Northern Virginia was engaged, it bore its steady and heroic share; and surrendered with Lee at Appomattox. As sure indication of the sort of fighting the company did, the following incomplete statement of the losses it sustained in some of the battles is given: First Manassas, 7 killed, 6 wounded, 40 present in the fight; Second Manassas, 3 killed, 7 wounded, 25 present for duty! Chancellorsville, 2 killed, 16 wounded, out of 28 present in battle. The casualties of the company in four years' service, 40 battles and contests in which it took part, were: Killed, 26; wounded, 59; died of disease contracted in the service, 15; captured, 46.

The company was recruited from time to time, so the total roll was 150 from the beginning of the war to the end. These recruits fairly maintained the reputation of the company achieved in its earlier engagements. Several of the company were transferred to other branches of the service, and one, Col. J. W. Reily, was promoted and assigned to staff duty. There were many instances of conspicuous gallantry on the part of individual members of the company. Badges of honor for distinguished courage were conferred upon privates George Chapin and N. A. Lackey, both of whom were afterwards killed in battle. Lieut. J. H. Jones and Private A. T. Barclay were commended, in general orders, for conspicuous gallantry; the former after the battle of Sharpsburg; the latter after Mine Run, and Private Barclay was promoted to the perilous office of ensign to the regiment. In the official report of the engagement at Mine Run or Locust Hill special mention is made of the gallantry of Private A. T. Barclay in the following terms: "Among the non-commissioned officers wounded is Color Sergeant J. H. Lawrence, who was severely wounded through both legs while gallantly bearing the colors of the regiment against the foe, and I desire to mention specially the conspicuous gallantry of Private A. T. Barclay, Company I, who seized the colors when Sergeant Lawrence fell and carried them through the balance of the fight."

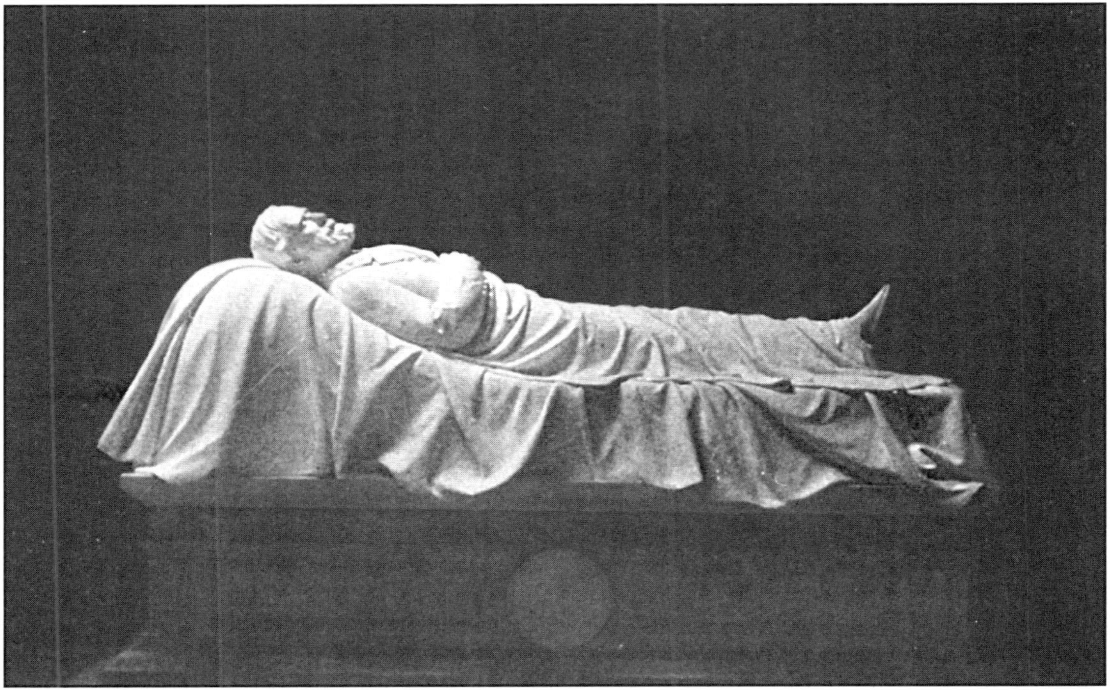

RECUMBENT FIGURE OF LEE.

OPPOSITE PAGE 60.

"20 *April*, 1896.

"MRS. ROBT. HULL,

"1020 Cathedral Street, Baltimore, Md.

"Dear Madam: Gen. Custis Lee, who is ill, desires me to answer your letter of the 17th inst. as follows:

"During the early part of the late war between the States there were many boys, under sixteen years, who entered the army; especially in the cavalry, artillery or as couriers to general officers. Many of them served to the end of the war if they were not killed in the mean time. After the passage of the conscript law, which gathered in all boys eighteen years old and upwards, there were still many boys who entered the army under the age of eighteen years. Gen. Custis Lee has sent you an account of the company of boys that went from this College ("Liberty Hall Volunteers") whose ages were stated, he believes, at either sixteen or eighteen. His brother, Robert E. Lee, Jr., must have been more than fourteen years old when he entered the army, as his father was very unwilling for boys to go into the field while there were so many grown men who could not be armed. Gen. Custis Lee is sorry not to be able to give you more information on the subject, but will gladly do so whenever he can.

"Respectfully,

"THOS. E. MARSHALL, JR."

HENRY E. SHEPHERD

Henry E. Shepherd was born at Fayetteville, N. C., and was at the University of Virginia when the war broke out. He left immediately and joined, as private, the first regiment organized in his State, and at eighteen years of age was elected first lieutenant of the Forty-third North Carolina Infantry under Gen. D. H. Hill and Gen. J. Bankhead Magruder. He served in the campaign in front of Richmond, 1862; was with General Hill in his movements against Newberne and Washington, N. C.; and in 1863 was transferred to Virginia and was in the vanguard of General Lee's army during the invasion of Maryland. At Gettysburg he was severely wounded in the attack upon Culp's Hill, his brigade having been detached from General Rodes to cooperate with General Johnson's division in that carnival of blood.

In this same engagement Capt. William Murray met his heroic death, Douglas was wounded, and Col. J. R. Herbert received three shots, one of which was most dangerous. After Mr. Shepherd was shot he lay for more than thirty minutes directly in the line of the Federal artillery, but was at last carried to an improvised hospital, his wound was dressed, and he had a cup of genuine coffee—an inexpressible luxury, as he had not tasted food for nearly three days, except a few cherries and some fossilized hard tack. He fell into the hands of the enemy on General Lee's retreat into Virginia, and was a prisoner for nearly two months in Baltimore in West Building, used as a hospital, on Concord street, near the docks. While in Baltimore he was subjected to every indignity and brutality; was marched in the broiling August sun from Camden Station to Marsh Market; suffered tortures from thirst and endured the agony of slow starvation. His letters were taken by the prison authorities, his friends kept from approaching him by the intervention of the bayonet—absolute terrorism prevailed in all directions. Nearly the only kindness he received was from the Catholic Sisters of Charity, who in certain hospitals had the care of sick and wounded. At last he found his way South and was paroled at the dissolution of the Confederate Army. He was complimented for gallantry on the field of Gettysburg, and despite his youth was personally known to our sovereign chief, Gen. R. E. Lee. He is now living in Baltimore in an important position and is an uncompromising Confederate, and holding the conviction that the justice and truth of the Southern cause are vindicated in the light of contemporary developments and are much more apparent in the political tendencies of 1904 than in the first stages of the struggle of 1861.

GEORGE BRINTON M'CLELLAN ENGLISH

Long before the Civil War there went from Alabama to Philadelphia, for his education, a young Southerner, Thomas English, the son of a rich cotton planter. While at college Mr. English met. wooed and won Miss Frederica McClellan, the beautiful and accomplished daughter of Dr. George McClellan, of Philadelphia. In her adopted State Mrs. English was surrounded with all the luxury that the landed estates could bestow in those antebellum days. She occupied the center of a large social circle in one of the most aristocratic cities of the South, her palatial home being located near the Alabama River and within a few hours' ride of the Gulf City (Mobile). Mr. and Mrs. English, with their children, frequently visited their Northern relations—the McClellans, of Philadelphia. In the spring of 1861 Mrs. English, with her children, were in the North, and when Fort Sumter was fired on were still north of Mason and Dixon's line. Her husband at that time was on his cotton plantation in Alabama. Lieut. George B. McClellan, Mrs. English's brother, had been made commander of the Army of the Potomac. In order to allow the reunion of the family an appeal was made to General McClellan, who allowed Mrs. English and her children to pass through the lines and join her husband at some convenient point south of the Potomac.

Thomas English became a captain in the Confederate company which was Gen. Braxton Bragg's escort. In the same company was Captain English's eldest son, George Brinton McClellan English, a youth of seventeen or eighteen years. Young English was captured, carried to a Northern prison, and while there his aunt, Mrs. McClellan, heard of it and sent him a box of luxuries, clothing and money to make him more comfortable in prison life, at the same time writing him that her interest was prompted only by love for a nephew and not for the cause he had espoused. Young George B. McC. English refused the kindness of his aunt and, it is said, returned the box and money, writing her that he would die before he would accept the gifts on her conditions. He did die in prison.

EXPLOIT OF SERGEANT SHANK AND HIS MEN IN '64

Dr. Carter Berkeley, of Staunton, contributes the following interesting war story:

In August, 1864, I, with a section of McClanahan's Horse Artillery, was encamped with General Imboden's brigade in Clarke County, a mile or two from the Shenandoah River. The Sixty-second Virginia was picketing at Berrie's Ferry, commanded by Colonel George Smith and Lieutenant-Colonel Lang, two magnificent officers. We had just returned from General Early's great march on Washington. Our command had been actively engaged all summer and the men pretty well worn out, and we were lying there quietly resting. Colonel Smith sent word to the General that everything was quiet on the river, but that he would like to have a piece of artillery sent to him. I only had one gun fit for duty. My other gun had been disabled a few days before in a lively little fight near Leesburg. I was in a very bad condition, so ill that I could not sit on my horse. The General knowing this, told me to send the gun down to the ferry in command of a sergeant, saying that there was no necessity for my going. I told Sergeant Shank to take the gun and report to Colonel Smith. He took with him a squad of young fellows from Randolph County, and a friend of his, Michael Henkle. I do not believe a braver body of men ever took a gun into action. The y had been with me at New Market, Piedmont, Lynchburg and many other battles, and I knew their worth.

The men of the Sixty-second were then lying under the shade on the banks of the beautiful Shenandoah, scattered along the river in a thin line. Some were mending their clothes, some sleeping, some smoking and fishing, and many of them writing letters to their people at home, but all had their arms by their side. The beautiful river was rolling sweetly and gently on to the sea. Everything looked calm and serene. Who would have thought that in a few minutes a scene so peaceful would be broken into by a bloody tragedy; that the beautiful blue grass would soon be stained with human blood, the velvety sod torn by the iron feet of charging squadrons, and the placid river filled with dead and dying men and horses! But such is war. Our sergeant had just about gotten in hearing distance of the ferry when he heard the rattle of musketry and the "Rebel yell" of triumph. The enemy had suddenly appeared on the other side, and a squadron of cavalry had made a dash across the ford to see what was there, and they saw; for they recrossed more rapidly than they had crossed. But not all of them.

The sergeant reported to the Colonel at once, and was told to select the best position he could and fire on the enemy, which he thought were in large force on the other side, and that the reconnoitering party would report how few men we had and would soon return in much larger force. Shank was on the road that ran down to the ferry. The water was low and now fordable. Just to his right was a ridge running parallel with the river and on it he took his position. To his surprise, when he got on it, he discovered the enemy's infantry and cavalry in large force massed in a bottom on the other side, in easy range of his gun. Without further orders, he opened on them, throwing with deadly aim shrapnel into the body of human beings. Men and horses went down at every fire; and the fire was rapid, for veterans were behind the gun. The Yankee general seeing that, unless that gun was silenced, his expedition would be a failure, ordered up a six-gun battery, and soon made it hot for the gallant little squad. The young hero saw that he must do something to save his men for the expected charge, so he made the men run the limber and the horses behind the crest of the hill, and ordered them to lie down and protect themselves. But in order to let the Yankees know that they were still on hand, he and his friend Henkle kept up a fire from the gun alternately. The Yankee general saw that he had to quiet that gun before he could make a successful charge across the river; so he ordered a regiment of cavalry next to the ford to dash across and capture the gun. They came on gallantly, riding over the thin line of infantry. Up the road they came, thundering with a shout of victory as they thought; turned to the left and dashed up the hill, expecting to take the gun in the rear. But sad and terrible was their disappointment.

The gallant and cool sergeant, seeing the intent of the movement, ran his gun by hand to a thicket just on the right, and when the enemy got to the place where they had seen the gun, they met instead a deadly shower of canister; and so rapidly was the gun served by those gallant Randolph boys, that the enemy fled back down the hill, every man for himself, trying to recross the river, which few of them ever did; for Smith had gotten his men together and was ready for them, and poured into their already depleted ranks a terrible fire, and not taking time to reload, knocked the fugitives from their horses with their guns. Shank rushed out from his position and captured two cavalrymen who had been dismounted. Each had a loaded six-shooter and forty rounds in his belt. Shank has one of the pistols now. The fight was over.

Imboden and General Bradley Johnson, hearing the firing, came as rapidly as possible to the assistance of the little band, but the Yankees had gone. Our young sergeant came down to the road, and was modestly standing there, seeming not to know that he had done anything great. He had shown himself to be a born soldier, not only brave, but a strategist.

As General Imboden rode up, Colonel Long said: "General, there stands the hero of the day. But for him, we could not have held the ford."

The General and other officers shook hands with him and congratulated him, and as the compliments were showered on him, he very justly began to feel as proud as did Wellington after the Battle of Waterloo. But he always gave the brave Randolph boys their share of the glory. When I heard the firing, I, as painful as it was, got on my horse and went to my brave boys as soon as I could. But it was all over. The work had been done, and well done. The General told me to send him a recommendation for Shank's promotion, which I did. He endorsed it and sent it to General Early; and he, no doubt, sent the papers to Richmond, where they stayed, as many others of the same kind had done. Our Government made a great mistake not to commission such men. Napoleon did it.

Samuel F. Shank is now living near North River, in Rockingham, and Mike Henkle in Augusta; and both are respected citizens.

The sergeant at that time was about eighteen years of age. His comrades will all testify that he always had the bearing of a soldier, a gentleman, and a Christian. In reviewing his conduct at Berrie's Ferry, I do not think it too much to say that what he did compared favorably with Stonewall Jackson's conduct when he won his first laurels at Cherubusco.

For the last two years of the war I had the honor to command a section in McClanahan's Horse Artillery. Most of the men under my command were from the Valley and from West Virginia. Their ages ran from about seventeen to twenty. General Lee once said that there never was a finer body of soldiers on earth than the Artillery Corps of the Army of Northern Virginia; that he had never known them under any circumstances to desert their guns. I can truthfully say for those young fellows who served under me, that they were always cheerful and obedient to orders in camp and on the march, and in battle they stood to their guns, even when death looked them in the face. I am proud to have been their commander and I believe that I have their love and affection; they certainly have mine from the bottom of my heart. And I pray that when the bugle sounds the last tattoo that we will all meet in the "Sweet bye and bye."

HENRY LLOYD TURNER

Henry Lloyd Turner, the son of Henry Turner and his wife, Susan Riddick Boush, of Norfolk, was at the Virginia Military Institute when the war broke out, and though only sixteen, left immediately and joined the Fifth North Carolina State troops, in which his first cousin, Samuel Flanegan, was a captain. Later he was with the V. M. I. Cadets when they were ordered to join Stonewall Jackson in his campaign up the Valley against Fremont and Milroy when the Battle of Bull Pasture Mountain took place and we followed them to Franklin in West Virginia. He was in the Battle of Seven Pines and in the Seven Days' fighting around Richmond to Malvern Hill, where he was incapacitated by an attack of typhoid pneumonia, followed by rheumatism. On his partial recovery he was sent to Baltimore on secret service for the Confederate Government and was there until nearly the close of the war. He had many narrow escapes from capture while in Baltimore as it was so closely watched and guarded, the United States Government knowing well there was nothing she would not do or attempt for the South, even though Maryland did not secede!

BENJAMIN TAYLOR HOLLIDAY

At sixteen Benjamin Taylor Holliday was so anxious to enter the Confederate Army that his father was induced to consent, and he with a number of very young boys from Winchester were brave and gallant soldiers—Wm. McGuire, Charlie Dandridge, the Glass brothers, and many others, all eager for the fray. I have been able to learn very few particulars of these boys, only general accounts of their dash and courage in the fight and the spirit of fun that helped them to bear the privations and sufferings of camp and march, never losing their manly honor and steady principle. After three years' hard service Holliday was captured and taken to Point Lookout, where he remained for twenty-two months. After the surrender he and a friend were carried to Richmond and there given transportation as far as Staunton on their way home. At Staunton a friend offered to borrow money to take him to Winchester, but Holliday declined, saying he did not know whether his family had anything left with which to pay the loan, as Winchester had been occupied for months at a time by first one army and then another. In his eagerness to get home Holliday walked the whole distance, ninety miles, in two days. His sister saw him coming in his old worn uniform, and said to herself, "I will ask this soldier-boy if he knows anything of my brother." The soldier-boy smiled and she recognized "Ben."

CARTER BERKELEY

Carter Berkeley was at the University of Virginia when the war broke out, and went with the Sons of Liberty to Harper's Ferry; but General Lee soon disbanded them and sent them home to raise other companies for the Army. He joined the Staunton Artillery, then commanded by Capt. John D. Imboden, and was recommended by him for promotion, but did not receive his commission until 1863. After the battles in front of Richmond he was transferred by General Lee to the Clarke Artillery, and after eight months' service with it he received his commission as lieutenant of artillery and orders to report to Captain, now General, Imboden. (His captain was a fine soldier but a very delicate man, and Lieutenant Berkeley was frequently in command of the company.) On his way he fell in with the Eighth Virginia, commanded by his brother-in-law, Norborne Berkeley, and fought with it in the Second Battle of Manassas.

Four Berkeley brothers were the four highest officers in this regiment. Norborne was Colonel, Edmund was Lieutenant-Colonel, William was Major, and Charlie, the youngest, was Captain. Every Berkeley in Virginia able to carry a musket was in the service. Only one was killed, but five were wounded at the battle of Gettysburg—four in Pickett's charge! After the Battle of Manassas one of the family met a Berkeley servant leading several riderless horses, and exclaimed in horror, "Where is your master?" "Dey is all killed, Missis!" he replied, weeping bitterly. One was killed and *all* were wounded.

In a letter from Lieutenant Berkeley he gives an account of three young soldiers: "My youngest brother, Spotswood, went into the Army with Frank Brooke at about sixteen, and both joined my company, McClanahan's Battery. Spotswood began writing to me about it, and worrying mother long before he was sixteen, and she told him whenever I said so he might go in. So he wrote me an appealing letter, promising to give me all the money he had and to carry water for me as long as the war lasted! [Spotswood Berkeley in his first letter to his mother said, "You need not worry about me; the only service I have seen so far has been to hold the Captain's

CARTER BERKELEY.

OPPOSITE PAGE 70.

horse in a pouring rain while he paid a long visit to his girl."—Ed.] It was wonderful how the young boys in Virginia rushed to the front as soon as they were allowed, and well did they know it was no child's play, for every day they heard the roar of cannon and saw the dead and wounded being brought home. Many times my heart ached to see the little fellows lying stiff and stark, their faces to the front, and it was awful to see them carried to the rear mutilated and bleeding; but it was grand to see how their poor mothers bore it. My mother never wrote me anything but an encouraging and cheerful letter. Just after the Second Battle of Manassas I went to a house filled with wounded to look for a friend. I saw there two young fellows, brothers, one not sixteen, the other not eighteen, both badly wounded. They were sons of Colonel Doyle, from Staunton. Bob, the youngest, was a beautiful blue-eyed, rosy-cheeked boy. He was cheerful and asked me if I wouldn't beg one of the kind ladies who were waiting on him to get him a kitten or a puppy to play with. As I bade them good-by they both said, 'I wish we could see mama; do you think she will come?' I met her the next day on her way to her boys. She got there in time to see poor little Bob die under an operation. Jack recovered. Her husband was killed at Piedmont—shot and bayonetted after he fell, trying to rally his men."

EDWARD BOAG, AN ENGLISH BOY

After one of the great battles, Fredericksburg I think, several wounded were brought to my division of the Winder Hospital, and my heart was with each one as he was lifted from the ambulance and laid on the floor until the surgeons could examine him before being put into the clean clothes and beds we had prepared. I noticed particularly two boys, both wounded in the head, and like the others covered with mud and blood. The smaller was so enveloped in bandages that not a feature of his face could be seen, but there were two naked feet, small and well shaped, as were his dirty hands. His pulse beat so feebly that I begged a passing doctor to tell me if there was still life. He replied, "Don't you see he is so wounded that he would be deaf, blind, and perhaps dumb should he live, for the bullet shattered his jaw, passed through his eye and came out at the ear. It is better he and his comrade go to the dead house." But I would not. Inserting a small tube, a pipe stem, in the corner of his mouth I poured in a drop of milk toddy, and as it did not ooze out I knew it had been swallowed. So every time I passed on my rounds I gave him another drop, and stopped a moment to pick the gravel and mud from his bleeding feet. Eventually we got him washed and in bed, over which was placed "unknown." For three months he lay without speech, hearing, or sight. Meanwhile an advertisement appeared in the Northern papers asking for information of an English "lad" named Edward Boag, whose mother had been a South Carolinian, and who in a moment of enthusiasm had run away from his English school to fight for his mother's country. There was no clue to his whereabouts but that he had enlisted in a South Carolina regiment as color-bearer. The hospitals were searched for "Eddie Boag" in vain, though our medical director (who was of the same family) came himself, but did not recognize the poor unconscious boy. When he came to himself he told us he was Edward Boag, and he was sent by flag of truce to his father in New York and taken to England. He sufficiently recovered to persuade one of his South Carolina cousins to marry him, and yet lives, or did live, in Brooklyn.

UNKNOWN

The other little fellow died in a few hours, never having recovered his senses.

UNKNOWN

At the hospital one day there was a poor little boy of fourteen to have his leg amputated at the thigh. I went to him and said, "My dear, there is great danger attending this operation. Don't you think you had better make your peace with God?" He answered, "I have made my peace with God long ago." I then asked him if he was a member of the church, and he said, "No; but when a boy dies in defense of his country he has made his peace with God already." The doctors, who were feeling his pulse all the time, said it never wavered or fluttered while the dreadful preparations were being made,—the instruments, the blood and all the horrible paraphernalia,—adding, "This is the stuff of which heroes are made."

I could fill a volume with incidents like these, dear Mrs. Hull, but spare you.

Most truly yours,

E. V. Mason.

My Dear Cousin:

I persuaded a daughter of Steve Timberlake, one of the best of our boy Company B, and one of seven gallant Timberlakes in it, to give me this incident and picture for your book if you want it. He has modestly forborne to tell of the part he took in the sabre-fighting with the detachment in the woods, on the occasion spoken of.

Your affectionate cousin,

THOS. D. RANSON.

A STAGE-COACH EXPERIENCE

In February, 1863, our brigade, Ashby's cavalry, was encamped near Mt. Jackson, and my company, Twelfth Virginia Cavalry, had been sent to picket a back road, left of Woodstock. After picketing one week we were ordered back to the regiment, but seven of us, Warner McKown, David Hewitt, George Timberlake, James L. Timberlake, James H. Timberlake, "Abe" Gordon and myself, knowing that Milroy's army was then at Winchester, concluded to make an independent raid on his rear. Following the mountain range, we traveled all that day and night until three o'clock, halting at the edge of a wood. Tired out we put our blankets down and went to sleep. When we awoke at noon the next day we were much surprised to find ourselves covered with a layer of snow about six inches deep. We went to supper that night at the home of one of the boys who lived nearby, and though it began to sleet and rain, we kept on and had not been gone fifteen minutes when a company of Yankees sur-

STEVE TIMBERLAKE.

OPPOSITE PAGE 76.

rounded the house looking for those "blamed Rebels."

That night about twelve we reached Smithfield, and the next day, as we were pushing along the Winchester turnpike, we learned at a blacksmith's shop that a stage-coach carrying Federal soldiers and U. S. mail was expected to pass about sunset. Determining to tackle it we retraced our steps and soon heard it coming. We surrounded it and gave the command to halt. On top, besides the driver, were two or three soldiers, and within Milroy's adjutant-general, the paymaster, and several others. We afterwards learned that the paymaster had over $100,000 with him. When we ordered them to surrender they hesitated for a moment, but our pistols were persuasive.

As we were unhitching the stage horses to mount the prisoners we heard another stage approaching, and leaving one of the boys to guard the prisoners we went to capture the other coach, which we did. By this time it was quite dark and one of the prisoners managed to escape unseen, and procuring a horse from a friendly Quaker on the road he soon informed Milroy of what had happened. Milroy at once ordered out two regiments, one to take the road west of Winchester, the other the Millwood Pike, both regiments to post a squadron at every cross road so as to intercept us. In the mean time, after securing our booty and prisoners, we started across the country, reaching the Millwood Pike at the "Old Chapel," two of us acting as advance guards. We then pushed on toward Millwood, feeling pretty confident; but our state of mind soon underwent a change, for as we neared the village we came upon two companies of Yankee soldiers.

"Who comes there?" we were challenged.

"First New York," we replied.

"Advance, First New York!" they ordered us.

"You advance!" we insisted.

After parleying for a while their captain gave the command to charge. Thinking "discretion the better part of valor," we two turned heel and fled, soon overtaking the others. In a moment the Yankees were upon us and our prisoners rolled off into the road while we made good time back toward the "Old Chapel."

One of our number, young David Hewitt, of Howard County, Maryland, as gallant a fellow as ever lived, was soon overtaken, as his horse was lame, and refusing to surrender was shot down and instantly killed. Another boy, George Timberlake, was taken prisoner, as he had changed horses with one of our prisoners who complained of great discomfort. He was riding one of the bare-back stage horses, and in attempting to dodge a sabre cut rolled off on the ground. The Yankee captain by this time had gotten ahead of his men, and having emptied his pistols was using his sabre. Still another of our fellows was doomed to suffer, the captain laying his face open from ear to the mouth.

[It was Timberlake, who, rallying from the shock of the blow, and before the captain could strike a second time, shot and killed him instantly.—Ed.]

The captain was then killed, his death putting an end to the pursuit. The prisoner, George Timberlake, was taken to Winchester, and the next morning sent for by Milroy and closely questioned.

"What route did you take to get into my rear?"

"I refuse to answer."

"How many, then, were in your party?"

Refusing to answer these questions, Milroy ordered him put in chains. At this moment one of the officers present stepped forward, asking to speak. He was the adjutant-general, with whom the prisoner had exchanged horses.

"General," said he, "let me speak a word in behalf of this man. I am under the impression that he would not be here now had he not very kindly exchanged horses with me in my discomfort." This speech caused Milroy to revoke the order about the chains and to have him treated as a prisoner of war. He was sent to Camp Chase, Ohio. The rest of us, who had escaped, started back to our regiment. On the way we forded the Shenandoah River, the cold being so intense that our clothes were frozen stiff by the time we reached the farther bank. When we arrived at Mt. Jackson and reported to our company, Colonel Asher Harman at once put us under arrest, or as our lieutenant expressed it, "Boys, just consider yourselves under arrest."

For the next two weeks, before the convening of the court martial, we lay around camp, free from all duties and enjoying ourselves generally. At the end of that time we were ordered to appear before the regiment at dress parade to hear the verdict. Our penalty was to have extra duty every other day for two weeks. At this point our colonel stepped forward and addressed us as follows:

"You are good boys," he said, "and have suffered too much already. I relieve you of this sentence. Report to your company for duty."

S. D. TIMBERLAKE.

NEW MARKET

ADDRESS BY JOHN N. UPSHUR, M. D.

I have heard the authorities blamed for allowing boys of such tender age to be exposed to the perils of battle. But this is unjust. In March, '64, a mass-meeting of the Corps passed resolutions offering its services to General Lee. His response was to the effect that if the Corps left Lexington he would be forced to send another regiment there; he would therefore prefer that it should remain, but that if its services should be required, it would be called on. This was the reason for Breckinridge's order to join his command at Staunton, which came the following May, and that led up to the participation of the Cadets in the Battle of New Market. * * * *

To understand fully the condition involved in the arrangement of Breckenridge's line of battle and the position of the enemy, it is necessary to know the topography of the country immediately in the neighborhood of New Market. This will enable us to appreciate more fully the consummate skill with which our great General handled his troops on that memorable day. You must bear in mind that on May 14th Sigel's forces had been engaged with Imboden below New Market, and that the latter had gradually fallen back, having taken some prisoners, some of which were seen on their way up the Valley, when we camped the same night. On the evening of the 14th Imboden had a conference with Breckinridge at Lacy's Springs. He was ordered to fall back slowly to draw Sigel after him, and precipitate an attack on Breckinridge's forces south of New Market, where he would have the advantage of selecting his position, as he was aware of the fact that the enemy's force was nearly three times that of his own. Imboden subsequently informed General Breckinridge that this plan had failed, that if he intended to fight he would have to come forward and attack. Colonel J. Stoddard Johnston, Breckinridge's chief of staff, describes the ground as follows:

"The turnpike passes down the Valley due north, through the town of New Market, which lies in a depression, where a small stream running west and crossing the pike at right angles cuts through the ridge and empties into the south fork of the Shenandoah nearby, which runs north and parallel to the pike. From New Market, both north and south, the country rises with gradual slopes, then in blue-grass pastures and wheat-fields, intersected with stone walls. The Massanutten Mountain runs parallel with the road on the east side, at the distance of a mile or two, with an intervening wooded valley, interspersed with wet-weather marshes, rendered by the rain then falling difficult for military operations, which gave our right good protection. On the west of the pike and parallel to it and about half a mile distant, runs the small branch of the Shenandoah, then swollen with the rains, a high ridge intervening, and ascending from the Valley by a gradual slope to the bluff banks of the river." Colonel Johnson further says: "Our line of battle rested with its right upon the pike and its left upon the summit of the ridge. We had but one line in two ranks, with no reserves. It was not long before our skirmish line became engaged, and our orders being to press the enemy, after sharp firing, Sigel's forces fell back to the summit of the slope about a mile to the north, and we occupied the town. This preliminary engagement was followed by heavy artillery firing on both sides, with comparatively few casualties, and consumed most of the forenoon. Much of the time it had been raining and the ground occupied by us being chiefly a wheat-field deep in mud, made it hard for our men, who had little or no rest during the night; and especially difficult for the handling of artillery."

It was subsequent to this time that the general engagement began, and the Cadets came into action. About noon the battalion was marched a short distance down the road, and then filing to the left, to the top of the hill, with a view to getting cover from observation and fire. This was about two miles to the south of New Market. There we halted, and the artillery, which had been stationed to the left on the crest of the hill, being unable longer to fire over our line of battle, and its movements hindered by the nature of the ground, passed to the front of us, going toward the pike, ten pieces under Major McLaughlin. It was these guns which subsequently did such execution, just to the east of the pike on our right wing. The two cadet guns were stationed in the road or just to the east of it. The battalion was then ordered to lie down behind a fence and load; subsequently, in about half an hour, we moved forward and took the place assigned us in line of battle, being the center and place of honor. Echols's brigade, consisting of the Twenty-second Virginia, Colonel Geo. Patton; Twenty-sixth Battalion, Colonel Geo. M. Edgar; Twenty-third Battalion, Colonel Derrick, was on the right resting on the pike.

Wharton's brigade, consisting of Fifty-first, Colonel Frostburg; Sixty-second, Colonel Geo. H. Smith; Thirtieth Battalion, Colonel Clark, all Virginia troops, was on the left, which rested on the crest of the ridge, the Sixty-second Virginia being immediately on the left of the battalion—Chapman's battery; Jackson's battery; and two 3-inch rifled Parrott guns served by Cadets under command of Cadet Captain Minge. These guns were served with distinguished gallantry. Colonel Edgar says that upon final formation he was ordered from right to the extreme left; as the line advanced, the front became too narrow because of the winding of the river, and he was forced to order a company at a time from front to rear, until his whole battalion was in the rear. When reaching the open ground, the regiment in front was subjected to such a galling fire that it was thrown into confusion, breaking through Edgar's battalion. Edgar ordered his battalion forward; the regiment rallied behind it, and returned to the fight. The artillery was so arranged by Breckinridge in person on the right, that as the line of battle advanced they should limber up, gallop to the front and open fire, making, as it were, a skirmish line of the artillery, frequently in front and to the right of the infantry. So exposed was the advancing line that none of the officers were mounted except General Breckinridge and his staff. The general impression prevails that there were two lines of battle, and the Federal accounts say three. But knowing that he was outnumbered, Breckinridge, fearing the enemy would overlap his flanks, in order to extend his line of battle formed it in echelon, thus giving the impression where overlapping came, just to the front of the Cadets, that we had two lines. A sharp artillery duel had been in progress for some time, when the line of battle was ordered to advance. Passing up the slope of the second hill, as we reached the crest, the enemy had gotten our range and the first casualties occurred, four or five men being wounded by the bursting of a shell, one of them being Captain Hill, of C Company. The line now pressed forward, the battalion being as beautifully aligned as if on dress parade. The ground here was an open field, level, or rising slightly to the north. When half way across this field, a sharp musketry fire opened on our left in addition to the artillery fire, and a shrapnel shot exploding killed three members of D Company: Cabell, Jones, and Crockett. Just at this point the wings of the battalion became advanced beyond the center, causing a curve in the line. The Cadets marked time, the line was straightened, and dressing on the center advanced in as perfect order as if on dress parade. On the northern border of this field and to our front, stood Bushong's house, beyond which was an apple orchard. The enemy had slowly fallen back and taken up a third position several hundred yards beyond this house. On reaching the house, the ranks divided, A and B Companies passing to the right of the house, and C and D Companies to the left; A and B marking time until the other half came up and the line was reformed. The fire at this point was terrific, both musketry and from the battery to our left, double shotted with canister. Passing beyond the house, the battalion laid down for a short time on the northern border of the orchard, when the order "forward" was given, and when about half way between this point and the guns, occurred the heaviest casualties of the day, the sufferers being the Cadets and the Sixty-second Virginia under Colonel Smith, immediately on the Cadet left. It was at this point that Colonel Shipp was wounded and Captain Henry A. Wise took command. Up to this time the Cadets had not fired a shot. At this juncture the Federal cavalry was seen about to charge the line, squadron front. Breckinridge, appreciating the situation, ordered the guns, double shotted with canister, turned on them. They were routed with great loss, only a few reaching our lines, and they as prisoners. Wharton's men seemed to have melted away under the terrific fire, leaving a gap in the line and producing some disorder. Falling back, they reformed behind the Cadets. Captain Wise ordered the Cadet battalion to advance to fill this gap, and a brilliant dash forward, gallantly seconded by the Sixty-second Virginia, and the battery was captured.

During the progress of the events just related, Imboden had discovered General Stahl with 2,300 cavalry massed in squadron front close order. He asked permission of General Breckinridge to allow him to uncover his right flank for a short time, in an effort to turn Sigel's left, which he thought he could accomplish. Receiving the desired order, in less than fifteen minutes he had gained a position behind a low hill unobserved by the enemy, six guns were ordered at a gallop to the crest of the hill, unlimbered and fired as fast as possible into the massed cavalry. The effect was immediate and terrific. The Federal guns, captured by the Cadets a little later, turned their fire in that direction to silence Imboden's guns, an enfilading fire from which aided materially the Cadets and the Sixty-second in the capture of the Federal guns. Meantime the Thirty-fourth Massachusetts, which was composed of seasoned veterans and which had been immediately to the left of the Cadets, falling back into a clump of cedars, was hotly engaged with Edgar's battalion, when Captain Wise moved the Cadets on their flank, and they broke and ran. Breckinridge halted his line to replenish ammunition before advancing on Rude's hill, about two miles below New Market, where Sigel made a final stand, and from which point he was using his guns. But he did not await the Confederate coming, but hastily retreated across the Shenandoah, burning the bridge after him—and the battle was won. I would call especial attention to the timely action of the Cadets in filling the gap in the line to which I have referred. It was the critical time of the fight, and a cavalry charge at that moment would have driven a wedge through Breckinridge's line, and we would have lost the day. So you can understand readily how the charge made by the Cadets at this critical juncture turned the tide of battle and crowned our arms with a success which meant so much. The enemy left their dead and many of their wounded on the field, besides several hundred prisoners, who fell into our hands, their total loss being from 800 to 1,500. Our loss amounted to about 400, killed and wounded, more than half of this having fallen on the Cadets and the Sixty-second. The Cadet loss being 8 killed and 48 wounded, out of 250 engaged—a larger proportionate loss than the Light Brigade at Balaklava.

General Breckinridge modestly telegraphed General Lee the result of the battle, and the same night received from him his thanks and those of the Army of Northern Virginia.

Colonel Otey says: "The Cadets came over the little crest in as beautiful a line as I ever saw on a parade ground. It was here I saw a shell plow through them, and then I saw them close up. Down to the valley they went and across the branch, until Breckinridge ordered the line to be reformed. Again a column of a regiment or so of Federals commenced to charge where the gap exists. But here the Cadets step in their way and utterly rout them. I speak by the card, for I was there, lying wounded between the two lines, and have no hesitancy in saying this saved the battle. I do not disparage these center boys, but they were in front before the line became one general line. They had had all the infantry fire and artillery fire. But they were cut up. They had done their part to press the whole force back till those in the rear echelons had joined them."

Another witness, Major Harry Gilmor, a participant in the battle, a man of large experience in war, and one not given to idle compliments, has said, in his "Four Years in the Saddle": "Breckinridge has gained, all things considered, the most brilliant victory of the war, achieved by small numbers against such fearful odds. Under his command was the Corps of Cadets from Lexington, under Major Shipp, composed of boys from fourteen to eighteen years of age. These boys fought like tigers, and earned the admiration of friends and foes. At one time they advanced on a battery stationed on an eminence covered with cedars, and supported by a full regiment of infantry. They were going up in perfect line, the colors a little in advance. The battery, of four pieces, was pouring canister into them, and two color-bearers were knocked down. When within four hundred yards, the infantry rose and opened upon them, Major Shipp halted and ordered them to fix bayonets, which they did under a terrible fire. While doing this Major Shipp was knocked down by a piece of shell, and lay for a moment breathless, but almost immediately was on his feet, and calling out to the Cadets, 'Follow my lead, boys!' started for the artillery, all of which he captured, together with a large part of the infantry, who said they felt ashamed that they had been whipped by boys."

Had Imboden succeeded in carrying out his orders to burn the bridge over the Shenandoah, the whole of Sigel's command would have been captured. Breckinridge captured six guns, five or six hundred prisoners, and a large number of small arms.

AN EYE WITNESS FROM THE OTHER SIDE

The following is a letter from Captain Franklin E. Town, late captain of the Signal Corps, United States Army, to an old Cadet of the Virginia Military Institute, and being from an officer of the Federal forces who witnessed the charge of the Cadets at New Market, it gives peculiar intrinsic value to this story of youthful bravery that will live in history as long as the proud banner of Virginia floats over the Old Dominion:

In compliance with your request that I would state what I observed of the action of the Cadet Battalion at the battle of New Market. Let me first explain, as briefly as possible. The Federal plan of the campaign of 1864, among other operations, contemplated a movement which would necessitate heavy detachments from the Confederate forces covering Richmond and Petersburg, and thus make more effective the attack which it was intended to make in due time upon that army.

Accordingly there was organized a corps, composed of about 8,000 or 10,000 men, under Major-General Sigel, and about the same force under Major-General Crook. The former to start from Winchester and proceed down the Shenandoah Valley, the latter to advance from West Virginia; the two detachments to unite at or near Staunton, Va., and thence proceed as one command to Lynchburg.

I was designated as chief signal officer of the corps or department, called "the Department of West Virginia," and in that capacity I marched with the division of General Sigel in the Shenandoah Valley. In preparation for this duty I had organized a command of some twenty-two officers and over two hundred enlisted men constituting the Signal Service force of the corps, and being well mounted, it formed a very respectable cavalry command. The foregoing is to explain my presence and opportunities for observation.

Our army was put in motion, I think, about the 10th of May, 1864, from our camp, a little south of Winchester. We moved down the Valley a few days, and on the morning of Sunday, May 15th, we left our bivouac, between Woodstock and Mount Jackson, and continued our march along the pike.

The Valley turnpike was then, and I presume it is now, a wide, smooth, macadamized road. Some rain on the previous day and evening had made the road a little muddy, so that the troops would naturally pick out the best spots to walk upon, and thus the column got to be a good deal "strung out." Following the troops was the artillery and then a long wagon train. Up to this time our advance had been opposed only by small skirmishing parties not strong enough to retard our march or to give battle.

Before noon on this day, information from the front was brought to General Sigel that the enemy was in position at New Market, about four miles from where the head of the column then was.

While I did not hear the conversation which ensued between General Sigel and his chief-of-staff, I think it was suggested to him to close up his column near to and fronting the enemy, and go into bivouac, and attack in the morning with the army rested and fresh; but I did hear General Sigel say loudly: "We may as well fight them today as any day; we will advance;" and he did push on the head of his column, all of infantry. I don't think any cavalry, and I am sure no artillery, was ahead of our position in the column.

After pausing a few minutes in a grove by the side of the road, and sending off some aides and orderlies with orders, during which time the infantry was passing us toward the front, General Sigel turned to me and ordered me to wait where I was with my command for the coming of Von Kleiser's battery, and escort it to the field, and then General Sigel rode forward to the battle. This battery was well to the rear of the column, and I think it was at the moment the nearest to the scene of action of any artillery in our command.

I waited about an hour, until the battery came up, when I closed in my command in front and rear of the battery, on the road, and brought it up to the field. When the battery went into position and unlimbered, the engagement was on; and indeed, I had heard the ring of musketry for some time previously. I presume there had been preliminary skirmishing, but I did not see it, for when I arrived on the field, the lines of our infantry were actively engaged with the Confederate infantry which were behind some light works.

Von Kleiser's battery went into position at the left of our line of battle, just on the crest of a low hill. My escort service being ended, my men were left a little in the rear and below the slight ascent up which the battery galloped to take position, but I rode up with my orderly to witness the operations, and sat on my horse, probably twenty or thirty yards to the left of the battery. The battery, which as I recollect consisted of four brass Napoleon guns and two twelve-pounder howitzers, opened fire at once on the Confederate lines. It was a good battery and its commander was very proud of it.

Being for the moment a spectator, I could see, and so could any one in position to see, that we were getting the worst of the fight. We had attacked with the head of the column while the rear was several miles from the field, and it appeared likely (as it really resulted) that we would be whipped before we got our troops on the field.

From the front of Von Kleiser's battery the ground sloped down, a very gradual descent, for several hundred yards, to a little ravine; an ideal ground for light artillery to fire over. The ground appeared unbroken, and it was green. It may have been a pasture, or more likely a field in which the crops were just springing up; but from where I stood it appeared like a smoothly-shaven lawn, and certainly from the muzzles of our guns to the ravine there was no shelter of any kind for troops advancing.

Standing on the crest of this slope after a short time, I observed a line forming in the ravine at the foot of the hill, which seemed about like a regiment in extent, but so "smart" and "natty" in appearance as instantly to suggest our own pet "Seventh Regiment" of New York City. They appeared more like militia on parade than troops in campaign. We very soon were able to identify the command as the battalion of the Virginia Military Institute, and certainly a more soldierly appearing corps never faced an enemy.

After perfecting their alignment this young regiment advanced toward our battery. It approached only a short distance when it halted and turned back, toward the ravine. There was no apparent disorder, nor did it seem that they were falling back in panic, but rather as if by some change of plan and in pursuance of orders.

The battalion remained but a short time in the ravine, and again advanced. They came on steadily up the slope, swept as it was by the fire of these guns. Their line was as perfectly preserved as if on dress parade or in the evolutions of a review. As they advanced, our guns played with utmost vigor upon their line; at first with shrapnel, then, as they came nearer, with canister, and, finally, with double loads of canister. As the battalion continued to advance, our gunners loaded at the last without stopping to sponge, and I think it would have been impossible to eject from six guns more missiles than these boys faced in their wild charge up that hill. But still they advanced steadily, without any sign of faltering. I saw, here and there, a soldier drop from their line and lie where he fell, as his comrades closed up the gaps and passed on. Their pace was increased from a quick-step to a double time, and at last to the charge, as through the fire they came on, and up to the guns, which they surrounded and captured; our artillerymen giving way when the bayonets, having passed the guns, were at their breasts.

I watched this action from my position, but a few yards from the left of the battery, and was so absorbed in the spectacle that it did not occur to me that I might possibly be included in the capture, until the presence of the enemy between me and the guns brought me to a realization of the circumstances, and I did not then consider it expedient to remain longer where I was.

History abounds in records of attacks and defences which stir the blood and command the admiration of all who can appreciate manhood, and chivalry, and heroism; but these tales are expected to be written of veterans, seasoned to battle in many campaigns. But when one stops to think that this charge was made by a battalion of young lads; boys, who there earned their spurs of knighthood before their lips were tinted with the down of a coming beard, the action looms up more grandly, and gives promise of future great achievements of men who, as boys, could do so well. As a military spectacle it was most beautiful, and as a deed of war it was most grand.

It is a trifle old saying, "blood will tell," but it is a true one. These young lads represented the best families, and carried in their veins the best blood of the South, and while every one of them could be faithful to the obligations of honor, even unto death, not one could falter in his duty. When such young men fall in a cause which they believe in, whether it is intrinsically right or wrong, one may realize the sadness of cutting off a life so full of promise, yet all—those who approved and those who opposed the cause they died for—will accord to them the tribute of sincere respect and admiration. The man who dares to die for his convictions will always be honored, and these young men placed their motive above criticism by their heroic belief in it.

It would seem to me most fitting that upon each anniversary of that action the Virginia Military Institute should tell to its young men the story of the heroism of their predecessors. Such deeds are an inspiration and incentive to great actions, and successive classes might well be pointed to such an example.

I don't believe the history of war contains the record of a deed more chivalrous, more daring, or more honorable than the charge of these boys to a victory of which veterans might well boast.

Very respectfully,

FRANKLIN E. TOWN,

Late Captain Signal Corps, U. S. Army, Tallahassee, Fla.

ADDRESS BY HON. JOHN S. WISE ON NEW MARKET DAY AT V. M. I.

Mr. Chairman and Comrades: The warmth of this greeting and your demand for a speech are both very gratifying; but I am not one of the scheduled orators of our festivities, and did sincerely hope that you would permit me to remain unnoticed in my humble place in the rear of the hall. I cannot claim a conspicuous share in the battle which we commemorate. I was one of the first five wounded. Capt. Govan Hill, Merritt, Read, Woodlief, and myself were knocked out by one six-pound shell in our first advance. True, I was delighted at the wound, and for thirty-nine years have bragged about it. All of us, in fact, have played that morning's work for all it was worth. But I may as well admit to you that in my heart of hearts I have always known what a small factor I was, and that whatever glory came to me from it was but the reflected light from comrades who bore the heat and burden of the strife.

Our battery halted on the Valley pike the day after New Market. General Breckinridge came by. He paused to compliment them. "Boys," he said, "the work you did yesterday will make you famous." Dave Pierce, sitting on his limber-chest, replied: "General, Fame's all right, but fur Gawd's sake where is your commissary's wagon? We like Fame sandwiched with bacon and hard-tack." I fear we are here, like Pierce, sacrificing our love of Fame to other passions.

I might call a goodly array of witnesses from my audience to bear witness that I was a very young and heedless, insignificant and trifling Cadet. I came here in the autumn of 1862, a pert child not sixteen years of age, and always believed that my father's object in sending me was to keep me out of the Army, for my oldest brother, the apple of his eye and the sweetest brother boy ever had, had fallen at Roanoke Island. It was pardonable if the brave old man sought thus to shield his little Benjamin. The thought makes his memory all the dearer to me, for he sacrificed all else to our cause.

General Smith, the father of the school, was Superintendent.

Scott Shipp, then twenty-four years old, was Commandant. Who of you has forgotten him and his dappled gray stallion? Who of you does not sweat freely at remembrance of his battalion drills? He looked older then than he does now. Somehow we feared him more. He was then the fiercest, oldest-looking young man, as he is today the gentlest, youngest-looking old man, we ever looked upon.

Colonels Preston, "Old Ball" Williamson, "Old Tom," and Gilham—"Old Gil"—were full professors. Colonel "Git" Massie, that marvel of mathematics, was an adjunct professor.

We buried Professor Stonewall Jackson.

The Assistants were "Tommy" Semmes, Henry Wise, "Bull" Robertson, "Abe" Scott, Govan Hill, Frank Preston, Marshall McDonald, and a host of others. Many of them, like Cutshaw, came here wounded to teach us until they were able to return to active duty in the field. Morrison was adjutant. In the summer of 1863 Cutshaw acted as Commandant, while Shipp was at the front.

Our first Cadet Captain was Dick Cunningham, followed in 1863 by Collie Minge, now a bloated cotton king; and he was succeeded in 1864 by Erskine Ross, now Federal Circuit Judge in California.

Our Cadet Adjutant was Cary Weston—dead and gone to his rest—as pretty a soldier as ever formed the Corps for battle or dress parade.

Who among you has forgotten "Duck" Colonna or "Patsy" Shafer or "Dad" Wyatt, the other Cadet captains of that day? Or Charlie Hardy—now in his grave—our color-bearer, fashioned like a young Greek god? Or quiet Woodbridge, sergeant-major, whose quality was never known to us until his battle pitch and poise revealed him as game as falcon flown from fist of king. Such were a few of our officers.

In our ranks stood the pride and flower of Southern homes throughout the length and breadth of the Confederacy.

I was slow to appreciate the serious obligations of a Cadet. In spite of loving and earnest admonitions, for a time I resolved to do as little as was possible without incurring the penalty of dismissal. When promotions were announced in June, 1863, I received none, to my great mortification. Then, for the first time, I realized that merit was the only means of advancement at the V. M. I. After a decided change for the better and a long probation, I was one day made corporal, vice Vaughan, resigned. It cost poor Frank Vaughan his life, for he was shortly afterwards killed in the service; but who shall tell the joy it brought to me?

At the Superintendent's office, a few days later, General Smith looked me over, and in his epigrammatic way said: "Ah! I see you are a corporal! Congratulate you. True, it is a small office. But we must all begin at the foot of the ladder. Napoleon was a corporal once. I was a corporal once myself!"

Now, boys, you who knew General Smith and know me, also know what I felt like saying—Thank God I did not say it.

But, oh, that corporal's rank! What joy it gave me. Of what mean tyranny it was the offspring. Before me I see one, two, three of my old rat-squad —Eubank, Cralle, and Tutwiler. I wonder where Baylor is? He was the fourth. They are all gray-headed men now. It has been a mystery to me through life why you four fellows, after you left this school, did not firmly, jointly, and severally, give me a sound thrashing for all my hectoring of you on yonder parade-ground. Yet, believe me, I thought I was doing God's service, boys, in trying to work up mighty ordinary raw material into fine Cadets. And, looking at you now, seeing what healthy and handsome old gentlemen you are, I believe you are indebted to me for much of your good looks.

Who else is here?

There is brave Cutshaw in the crowd. God bless him! When he was our Commandant he had a wounded leg. Afterwards he lost it altogether at Sailor's Creek, covering Lee's retreat to Appomattox. The Corps was in camp. I was but a private. The Colonel was courting a comely spinster in Lexington. Colonel, you were a very strict disciplinarian. Nay, sir, you were a very trying martinet! I fear you not! I speak the truth. He published orders confining the whole Corps to camp because some foolish neighboring farmers suspected us of partiality to their apples. We had an awful time removing that unjust suspicion from Cutshaw's mind. At last, by dint of much persuasion and entreaty, the order came to the guard tent relaxing the rigor of our limits. I was on guard. I thought I had seen Cutshaw leave the camp. Never doubting he was out visiting his dulcinea, I joyfully seized the order and running into the street aroused the camp with the shout, "Boys, turn out. The tyrant's heart is busted." To my horror the Commandant stepped forth from his tent, almost at my elbow, and ordered me to my quarters. I forget how our differences were adjusted, but satisfactorily, I know, for I have ever held him in the greatest affection and esteem. Much of the efficiency of the Corps at New Market was due to the faithful work of Cutshaw.

It so happened that one day in camp I knocked "Big" Evans in the head with a tent peg for reporting me for noise. Evans was right, but he got the tent peg in the jaw all right, and I got the guard tent. Evans was about six feet two. A fist fight between us to settle our dispute was impracticable, so I challenged him through my friend, "Goat" Chaffin, for a duel. He said he would fight me the duel if I'd write home and get my father's consent. As the difficulties in the way of that were obvious, the duel failed. I put Evans down for a coward until at New Market he behaved so gallantly that he was made first sergeant of our company in place of Cabell, killed. As the natural outcome of the tent-peg episode, Evans did not see in me very promising material for a sergeant when he was recommending the promotions of corporals, and if somebody else had not been good to me I would not have been a sergeant at all. As it was, but one sergeant was below me, and that was Ezekiel, now Sir Moses Ezekiel. Now Ezekiel is one of the greatest of living sculptors, but then I resented bitterly the fact that of all the sergeants he was the only one I ranked. The night after promotions were announced we all tramped from Lexington to Balcony Falls, the nearest point to which the canal boats could approach, after Hunter's raiders had destroyed the locks. My companion on that tramp was my roommate, cousin, and *alter ego,* Louis Wise, who is here today, having come all the way from Texas. It is the first time we have met since the ending of the war. "John," said he, in one of our confidences, "do you remember how you that night cursed Ezekiel as the only worse soldier than yourself in the Corps?" I do, indeed. I think we did not take ten steps that night without my recording some protest against the indignity. Not that I disliked Ezekiel. On the contrary, he was a good fellow and a bright fellow; but until that day I had thought I was a rattling soldier; thenceforth I proclaimed there was but one worse soldier than myself in the world, and that was Ezekiel. Well, I have forgiven Evans. He is a judge in California now. And now that we have come to unveil Ezekiel's glorious monument, I can say with truth that I am reconciled at last, and that I am even proud to mention the fact that I ranked him.

Who else have we here? There sits our brother, smiling "Old Gabe" Wharton, looking scarce a day older than he did the day he went in with his brigade on our right at New Market. What a steady fighting man he was. How he and his veterans inspired us! How generous, too, they were in praising us unduly when our work was done.

And here is Henry Wise, beloved of all of us. The same old Henry who led the Corps so gallantly when Shipp went down. The bravest and the tenderest, the loving, and the daring. Not since Thackeray gave us Dobbin has the world had another one like him. As he and Louis and I "clomb the hill together" last evening, from the depot to the town, just as we three mounted it in 1863, upon our return from Covington, after Averell's raid, imagine, if you can, the tender retrospect, the gratitude we felt that we had been spared through all these years to meet here once again. It made us boys again. And what think you we talked about in that sweet and solemn hour? "Louis," said I, "is not that orchard on yonder hill the one we robbed so often?" With his dim eyes peering uncertainly, at last the gleam of recognition came, and Louis, vestryman of St. James' Episcopal Church, Abilene, Texas, shamefacedly confessed beneath his breath, "I'm afraid, John, that it is." Henry affected a certain air of "I am holier than thou" until we reminded him of that night before New Market when he chided us for swearing and for chicken-stealing on the eve of battle, and then, himself, next day, not only forgot himself and "swore like our army in Flanders," in the thick of the fight, but, when it was over, shared with us, without a protest, the cold remnants of our stolen fowl.

Well, boys, may the Lord forgive us all our sins. And I believe He will.

Lo! There is little "General" Randolph in the throng. How well I remember the day he reported. He was the pet and courier of Stonewall Jackson! So young and brave that even Stonewall's heart was softened and sought to have him spared, by sending him here, to be our pet, for the love we bore his great commander.

Then came New Market, and the little General, in the forefront of the fight, fell with a ghastly wound, recovery from which was almost a miracle. Snatched from the very jaws of death, he recovered and dedicated his life to God, just as Stonewall would have had him do.

Oh! reverend man of God, whom it is a privilege to claim as comrade, who could more appropriately ask His blessing upon us? Who else would be so near to those for whom he prays?

And here is Fred Claybrook, second lieutenant of "D" Company, likewise a Christian minister. Verily, the lessons of the V. M. I. were not so fruitless of good results after all. May all of us be saved by these vicarious atonements.

Before me, too, I see a grave and reverend Judge. Not much of him physically, it is true, but in Norfolk they call him "*Multum in parvo.*" What more could be expected from "Mouse" Martin, the tiny marker on the colors?

And here is private Edmund Berkeley, of D Company, now railroad magnate traveling in his private car. How dare he come here putting on such airs in the presence of his superiors? It makes quiet Capt. Patsy Shafer, also present, hang his modest head in shame.

There, side by side, sit Frank Lee Smith, of Alexandria, and Preston Cocke, of Richmond, and Dick Tunstall, of Norfolk. High and mighty lawyers now are they; but to us only Cadets once more, of the old war Corps.

And here is Hugh Fry, looking even smaller than he did that day at New Market, when he looked like the little son of the big Dutch prisoner he came leading back. And "Big" Wood, of North Carolina, our color corporal, who helped to buck me on the day that I reported. And "Cooney" Ricketts without one trace of the "peach-blow" cheeks that set the girls wild about him.

So I might go on indefinitely, for, of the seventy-odd survivors before me, each has his own story, each his interesting individuality for me.

O Comrades of my boyhood's happy days—Boys! Softly I call the name, because my swelling heart scarce leaves me utterance. We are standing together once more, boys. Aye, we have come with hearts brimming with such love and such honor as children render to a mother whose wealth of care and wisdom has flowed to them as ungrudgingly and with the same sustenance as mother's milk. We yield our Alma Mater that loyalty as unreservedly as if by the constraining power of Nature. For here in her loving charge were passed our happiest days of boyhood together in an intimacy as close as that of brothers under the paternal roof. To her we owe this tribute, in common gratitude, even in the joyous hour of our heart-satisfying reunion. Let it go forth to our credit as well as hers, as part of our proceedings. Let the world see that in our heart of hearts she is enshrined as a Mother, ever fresh and fair.

As for our old selves, there is little more to add. If ever there were boyish bickerings among us, this day at least all such are swallowed up and forgotten.

Our hearts are beating in perfect unison, our eyes sparkling with friendship and contentment at thought of this, perhaps our last, parade.

So Hail, Brethren, and Farewell!

Yet ere I close, unworthy as I am, may I not ask this benediction?

May the good God, under whose guidance and protection we have passed through the dangers of our youth, the trials of our manhood, and have entered on the decline of age, still vouchsafe to you His mercy and hold you in blessed keeping. May He crown your declining years with peace and rest, in contrast with that opening of war and toil. May you be blessed with faith in Him, with health and happy homes and loving wives and children, and troops of friends, for many years. May death, when it comes, as it must, find you ready in consciousness of honorable life. And may the reviving thought of that glorious day of our boyhood, when, cheerfully and unconsciously, we did the work for which we are this day praised, linger fresh and green and comforting in our memories to the last gasp of life. And when we are gone, may our beloved Mother School continue on her proud career, cherishing our humble names as those of loyal sons. May the story of our little day be an inspiration to the youth of future times to seek the proud title of Cadet in the Virginia Military Institute.

NOTE.—One of the very young Cadets left behind when the others went to New Market, to guard the Institute, said that many of them wept bitterly at the "disgrace" of not being allowed to "fight for their country."

FROM "A BOY'S EXPERIENCES IN THE CIVIL WAR, 1860-1865."

When the Virginia Military Institute was burned after the battle of New Market where the Cadets lost a number who were killed and where many were wounded, the corps was sent to Richmond. Every Richmond boy had a great ambition to go to the Institute, at that time regarded as the West Point of the South. The Cadets were a part of the Confederate Army and every graduate was given an officer's commission in the Army. Incidents were constantly occurring to keep alive and active this spirit to become a cadet—boys have little fear of bullets, they enjoy the excitement of active army life and even death and wounds appeal to them as making heroes. After the battle of New Market one of the Cadets, a son of Dr. Cabell, of Richmond, who was killed in that battle, was brought to Richmond for burial and his funeral took place from his father's home on Franklin street where he lived, a neighbor of General Lee. I remember as the remains after the service were borne down the front steps and through the iron front gate the intense awe and respect in the face of the young men assembled on the pavement around the entrance to the open space in front of the house. It was here I believe I first formed the determination to be a Cadet, and strange to say when I first entered the Cadet ranks, the drill master assigned to our squad was Bob Cabell, a brother of the Cadet whose funeral I had attended that day.

The Cadets of the Virginia Military Institute were in number about five or six hundred, were from all over the South and ranged in age from about sixteen years to about twenty-four or five. I entered the Institute shortly before the evacuation of Richmond and enjoyed the dictinction, as I have stated, of being the youngest Cadet in the corps. When the Cadets first came to Richmond, they marched with singularly soldier-like precision and carriage out Grace street to the Fair grounds, where they were for a time quartered. The uniforms of the boys, as also their food, began to partake of the Confederate soldier variety, and it was pathetic to see some of these boys marching in ranks through Richmond to their quarters with pants torn or worn out at the bottom and variegated in outfit, some with cadet jackets and plain pants, others with cadet pants and plain jackets. The Richmond Almshouse was assigned to the Cadets for their quarters. Life there would have been ordinarily recognized as singularly trying; to the young men in the corps it was a perpetual joy, alloyed alone by the obligation to attend lectures. The rooms that were a delight to them were simply unmentionable. In my room, about twelve feet wide and twenty-four feet long, were sixteen Cadets, who slept and studied there. In the daytime the mattresses were piled each on top of the other in a single corner of the room—at nighttime they were arranged side by side with head against the wall. One long table occupied the center of the room. It was supposed to be a study-table and was occupied at night by a favored one to sleep upon. In the daytime it was never occupied, except by the boys lounging upon it in lieu of chairs, smoking their pipes and gossiping. Pure atmosphere day or night in that room was not needed by those

VIRGINIA MILITARY INSTITUTE.

OPPOSITE PAGE 106.

young men with their wonderful vitality. At night-time the door was invariably kept closed by any who were up playing cards or gossiping after the retiring hour to shut out from view the officer of the guard, who whenever he wished to investigate for such breaches of discipline always discreetly and considerately knocked before entering, opening the door to find everything in perfect order. Each room had a petty officer, usually a corporal, a senior, who was supposed to be responsible for the good order and cleanliness of the room. One of the duties of this senior was to initiate by "bucking" any new Cadet introduced into his room. This "bucking," peculiar to the Institute, consisted in taking the newcomer's right hand, carrying it behind his back, twisting it around until he was compelled thereby to bend over, when he would be struck by the senior with a bayonet scabbard on his posterior once for each letter in his name, and in the event he was without a middle name he was given the right to select one, and upon failure to do so was given the name Constantinople for its many letters. Thereupon he was dubbed a "rat," which name he bore for one year. He was liable to have trouble for the whole first year and might have to take another bucking or stand up to a fight, which usually was brought about in a formal way and was a great affair. The corporal of our room was a mild-mannered, gentlemanly fellow named Bayard, of Georgia, whose father was, I believe, in the Confederate Congress from that State. After bucking me and permitting me to choose Asa for my middle name he dubbed me "mouse," and stated to me that if any one attempted to give me any trouble to let him know.

No trouble was there though for me—it was one constant stretch of delightful experiences. The association with older boys and men, who treated me not simply as an equal but from my youth and boyishness showed me every favor, rendered my life one of joyous ease. I was informed by the Cadet whose name immediately preceded mine in roll call of my company that any time I wanted to get off to let him know and he would answer twice, once for himself, once for me. I was introduced by a friendly Cadet to the apothecary's assistant, who turned an honest dollar in selling surreptitiously to the boys ginger cakes and pies at a thousand per cent. profit. I was recommended to old "Judge," the negro head cook and steward, who, black as coal, was with the boys the most popular person in the corps; but for his favors, which usually comprised an extra allowance of bread, expected a suitable remembrance. A room I have here described could furnish no more than living quarters for the number occupying it, and how any studying could be done at night by two dull tallow candles, the only lights, was inexplicable. Toilets were performed in a general wash-room, adjoining a larger room, where all trunks were kept, and these two rooms were on the same stoop or porch and a little apart from the living-rooms that all adjoined. If meagre fare contributed to good health, the boys were entitled to the extraordinary health they possessed with such surroundings. A typical breakfast was "growley," bread and Confederate coffee. Sometimes sorghum molasses took the place of "growley." This latter dish was quite watery, being a hash of beef, potatoes, and onions. A typical dinner was boiled Irish potatoes, boiled corned beef and bread. Meals were served in the large dining-room in the basement at plain pine tables with no covering, each table seating about one dozen. At the head of the table stood the large dish of "growley" or the corn-beef, and at each Cadet's plate was his half loaf of bread. It required practice and expertness to slide one's tin plate over the table to the "growley" dish for a helping, and some art to secure at long distance the favorable disposition of the Cadet sitting at the head to whom fell the delightful emolument of apportioning the "growley." The half a loaf of bread was where old "Judge" came in, for you always felt as if you wanted more. Each Cadet was furnished his own two-pronged fork and a good large table knife, both of the rough, bone-handled variety, colored a dark brown. This fare with undue discipline would have been unbearable, but with the free and independent life led there it was only a pleasing passing incident in the daily routine of Cadet life constantly filled with ever recurring incidents to surprise, interest, and exhilarate, and no grumbling ever took place, only high spirits and the fullest animal enjoyment in the flush of health.

A bell rang for classes or lectures and the class-rooms were a wonder. The classes were so large that many would have to stand up grouped together, usually near the door. Before the lecture was finished the groups would be greatly thinned out, for from time to time while the professor was absorbed in his work or inspecting the black-boards the door would softly open and out would slip some member of the group, who would softly close the door and walk past the windows of the class-room as naturally as if he were on a mission, the only evidence of irregularity being the exceedingly expert quick way with which he vanished through the door. Another result of the large classes was the effort to test the students by requiring several to recite at once, as one at a time would never have reached around. This was supposed to be accomplished by means of the blackboard. At each of the five or six boards was stationed one cadet and the same test was furnished to all at once. Out of the entire number at work usually at least one knew his task well. The others made a show of great industry and with much waste of chalk and many changes and corrections and with a sharp eye on his neighbor's work he managed to construct a passable performance. The last exhibit I saw in the geography class was a curiously drawn map in chalk outlining South America. It was not difficult to identify the copies of various grades and conditions, nor the original from which made. I suppose the professor was charitable in not holding his students to a too strict accountability. I wonder, indeed, how they could do any studying with such conditions or surroundings, instead of showing the general faithfulness that they did to their work.

As I have stated, a fight was a very formal affair; while usually originating in quite an unmentionable way it was arranged to take place with a full regard to the proprieties. One of the sixteen men in my room was a boy named Lovenstein, from Richmond. He was a new Cadet like myself and was therefore liable to have trouble. He had declined to submit to some indignity required of him by an older Cadet and he was thereupon challenged to fight. This latter he had no way of escaping. It was passed around during the day that there was to be a fight in so and so's room that night. I got there in company with the men from our room about half after eight o'clock, the hour these affairs usually occurred. The room was packed to suffocation, standing around an improvised ring. The air was filled with tobacco smoke but there was absolutely no talking or noise. In the ring in the center of the room the two fighters were facing each other. My sympathies were with Lovenstein, because he came from our room. Lovenstein stood up manfully to his task, with the creditable result that secured for him the regard of the other inmates of our room, and it soon became understood that he was to be protected thereafter and that no further trouble was to be put up for him.

The gala performance of the day was at dress parade. This occurred at five in the afternoon. The large plaza fronting the full width of the Almshouse furnished a fine parade-ground. Colonel Shipp, a portly, dignified, impressive man, who at the time of my present writing is still at the Institution, now as Superintendent, was then the Commandant. His adjutant was named Woodbridge, and these two, with the well-drilled corps, as a whole furnished the three striking incidents of the parade. The awkward squads, consisting of new Cadets, were put through simple evolutions at the same hour off from the parade-ground at each end of the building. Visitors in large numbers assembled to watch each drill of the corps. At the close the Cadets were at liberty to stroll off in the neighborhood for an hour's recreation, and that was liberally availed of. Soldierly dignity was not invariably preserved in these strolls. Pent-up youthful vitality freed from restraint showed itself in rough play, and upon one occasion an older companion of mine, in the exuberance of his spirits, lifted me to his shoulders and completed his walk, bearing me with him in this position until his return to the restraining formalities of the Institute grounds. One's introduction to the Institute was in strict military discipline; the details of name, age, residence and the taking of the oath of allegiance to the State and to the Confederacy were followed by a written requisition for a blanket, mattress, knife and fork, etc., and an assignment to a room and company. Mine was B Company. A sedate and dignified-looking Cadet named Ross was captain; a good, old-fashioned, friendly fellow named Royston was orderly sergeant. My introduction to the corporal of my room was through an army officer, Captain Shriver, who had recently graduated and who accompanied me and my father on my entrance into the Institute.

General Smith, the Superintendent, was only seen by the Cadets in his private office at the far end of the building. The only visit I made to him was quite an event in my life. Usually visits to the Superintendent were quite serious affairs, furnishing checks to exuberant spirits, often grave in consequences. Therefore a notification that your presence was desired by the Superintendent was calculated to set the heart going more rapidly and to stir the memory for some breach that must have been discovered. The summons to me one day just as I was about to attend my French lecture was as unattractive as attending the lecture. But when I reached the Superintendent's room I found there three Confederate soldiers, constituents of my father's and friends of my family, who had come out to see me and had secured permission for me to accompany them back to Richmond to spend the day. An event of the day was the taking of a photograph in a group. This, with a good supply of peanuts and a visit to the theatre, furnished quite a full day for us four—three seedy and friendly Confederate soldiers and a youthful Cadet just fourteen years old. Their request to General Smith to allow me to accompany them on their lark had evidently appeared so unique that I was struck with the degree of pleasure it seemed to afford him and my soldier friends.

The meagre fare made me yearn greatly to participate of the food that I knew was being enjoyed at my home, and I was not slow in availing myself of any temporary leave I could obtain. One of these occasions took place just shortly before the evacuation of Richmond, and upon my return to the Institute I was greeted by an almost empty building. I found the Corps had been called out the night before to go to the front, leaving me as a younger Cadet with a number of others as a detail to guard the Institute. For the short time we were in charge there were of course no lectures and little discipline, each one could go and come as he chose, with the result that my visits to my home board were more interesting, and in my saunters along the streets I began to notice on the Saturday prior to the evacuation premonitions of coming trouble. Great activity was suddenly manifested through the various Confederate Government departments. The Cadets at the Institute were extended permission to remove their trunks. This was availed of on Saturday and also on Sunday, until the Institute was practically abandoned by every one there; but was filled with the furniture and the trunks of all the absent Cadets, except of those few who had friends to take charge of them. Besides my own trunk I was able to care for that of another room-mate and sent it to him by express to his home some weeks later.

On Sunday morning, the 2d of April, 1865, it was apparent to any one that the city was to be abandoned by the Confederate troops. Great piles of official documents and papers of all sorts were brought out from the departments, piled up in the center of the streets in separate piles at short distances apart and then set on fire to be destroyed. Some few burned entirely, others only smouldered and others again failed to burn at all. The result seemed to depend on the quality of the paper and the density of the bundles. From one pile I took out a roll of Confederate bonds with all coupons attached and from another pile a bundle of official papers of various sorts. On Monday morning, the 3d of April, I saw going up Marshall street about daylight two Confederate cavalrymen on foot, who were the very last of the Confederate soldiers to leave Richmond. On the same morning about eleven o'clock I saw the first Union soldier to enter Richmond. He was also a cavalryman, riding up Broad street, and was near Tenth street when I saw him, and was surrounded and followed by a howling, frantic mob of about five hundred negro boys, there being no other person except myself that I could see on the street in the vicinity. Between these two periods, the going of the last Confederates and the coming of the first Union soldier, stirring scenes were being elsewhere enacted. I had first gone out to the Institute to see how matters stood there and I found it was in possession of a horde of men, women and children from all the neighborhood around, who had broken open the building and were carrying away everything movable—furniture, cadets' trunks, books, guns and swords—indeed, their vandalism spared nothing. I went to my room and was able to secure my blankets and my knife and fork and my books. It was intensely distressing to observe the property of the Cadets, who were off in the discharge of their duty, boldly appropriated and carried off before my eyes by these multitudinous freebooters, who preyed upon it as if it was so much public spoils free to all who chose to help themselves.

LIEUTENANT CARTER BERKELEY'S DESCRIPTION OF BATTLE OF NEW MARKET

[Lieut. Carter Berkeley was a member of the Sons of Liberty, sergeant in Imboden's battery, member of the Clarke Cavalry (Company D), Sixth Virginia, and lieutenant in McClanahan's Horse Artillery.]

Imboden's brigade and the Cadets bore the brunt of that battle, and their loss was greater than the combined loss of all the other commands on our side that were engaged in the fight.

Mr. John S. Wise, in giving an account of the part the Cadets took in the battle, does not mention either that Imboden's brigade or McClanahan's Horse Artillery, which was attached to that brigade, was actually engaged all day.

In winding up, Mr. Wise says: "The broken columns of the enemy could be seen hurrying over the hills and down the pike toward Mount Jackson, hotly pursued by our infantry and cavalry." The fact is that General Breckinridge had no cavalry at hand at that time, and used the artillery to drive the enemy off Rood's Hill, where they had attempted to rally. I have a letter from Col. Stoddard Johnston, General Breckinridge's chief of staff, who says that the General had sent all his cavalry around to the right to get in the rear of the enemy on the pike below Mount Jackson, and consequently had to use his artillery instead.

I commanded a section of McClanahan's battery, and with it, under General Breckinridge's immediate command, opened the fight early in the morning on the left of the village, and disabled the first gun that came out to reply to us just beyond the village on the pike.

"After firing from that position for some time the General ordered me to take a position, which he pointed out, on the other side of the pike. As we crossed the road in obedience to his order we for the first time saw the Cadets. They were standing near some wagons, and, as we thought, acting as a rear-guard. Among them were several Staunton boys, whose names I will give as nearly as I can remember—Carter H. Harrison, Alex. Stuart, John Stuart, Travis Phillips, Carrington Taylor and Jacob Imboden. We also had some Staunton boys in McClanahan's battery—Lieut. H. H. Fultz, Orderly Sergeant Joe Meriken, Sergt. James W. Blackburn, E. C. Kinney, F. T. Brooke, A. S. Berkeley, Silas Trayer, Sandy Calvert, John Garber, John Peer, Henry Carter, Dick Ryan and J. McC. Woodward are all that I can remember at this time.

Some of these boys were between the ages of sixteen and eighteen, and recognizing their old friends and schoolmates among the Cadets, began to jeer and guy them as soldiers generally did in passing each other, but of course all in a friendly way, halloaing at them "Bomb-proof!" "Wagon dogs!" "Get out of them good clothes!" The Cadets, not being accustomed to that sort of thing, became very indignant, and would have resented it if we had stayed with them long enough for it.

We soon arrived at our position, and from it we could see the whole field. Before we could get unlimbered for action, a Yankee battery opened vigorously on us from across a ravine in our front, and we replied to them as soon as we got in form.

Over on my left I could see our men forming in line to charge, and, to my surprise, I saw the Cadets coming into the line of battle, the Sixty-second Virginia, of Imboden's brigade, commanded by Colonel Smith (an old Cadet), on the right, with Echols's brigade on their left. I called to my boys: "Look yonder at your bomb-proof friends, how beautifully they are going into action; let's help them," and I gave the command to limber up and move farther to the front, so that we could very nearly enfilade the enemy's battery in front of our centre.

"Soon the deadly work began, and our boys would cheer every time our shells would strike in the Yankee line. It was grand to see how beautifully and steadily the young heroes moved to their work; a short time before tender-hearted youths, now inspired by the Rebel yell of the old veterans on either side of them to the glory of battle, they bared their breasts to the deadly storm, as iron-hearted as the men who followed Lewis Armistead over the stone wall on Cemetery Hill.

Just at this time one of the most terrible storms I ever witnessed arose. You could hardly distinguish the loud clap of thunder from the roar of over thirty pieces of artillery which were then in action. A dark and angry cloud hung over the combatants, the forked lightning flashed through the blackness as if heaven were crying out against the horrid work which was going on. The cloud was so dark that as our devoted men came closer to the enemy's line the blaze that belched from the guns flashed in their faces.

The two lines had now gotten so close to each other that I gave the command to cease firing, and we all stood with breathless silence anxiously waiting for the result of the charge. Then when we heard the triumphant yell of victory as our line of battle went over the enemy's guns and saw their support breaking in confusion our joy knew no bounds. Our boys fell on the ground, kicked up their heels and yelled with perfect delight. The victory was won. But, oh, at such a cost! "The Bourbon blood, how it flowed!" The Cadets had left in their rear, weltering in their blood, 56 killed and wounded, out of 250 in action; the Sixty-second, 245 out of 550. One company (Woodson's) lost 55 out of 60. Just then the rain began to pour down in such torrents that our advance was temporarily stopped, which gave the retreating enemy a better chance to escape.

In a few minutes a courier dashed up and told me that General Breckinridge said that I was to bring my guns to the pike and report to him at once. I followed the courier through our line, and found the General sitting on a splendid Kentucky horse, looking like the very god of war, and as I touched my hat to him he said: "Lieutenant, are your horses fresh and strong?" I replied: "Yes, sir." He said: "I have no cavalry, unfortunately. I sent it all with General Imboden to get in the rear of the enemy on the pike beyond Mount Jackson. I fear they are taking advantage of our stop to make a stand on Rood's Hill."

The rain had decreased considerably in volume and we could see the enemy on either side of the road, on the hill which was, I think, about a mile off. Just about that time one of their guns opened on us. The General said: "Go at once; charge down the pike and drive them off the hill. I will follow up with the infantry as rapidly as possible." I rode at once to the pike, where I had left my guns, and found that Lieutenant Collett had joined them with another section of our battery.

We had six guns, but two of them had been knocked out in the fight the evening before. Our boys were highly elated at being selected to do a thing so daring and so unusual, and as soon as I gave the order we put out at a run, every man yelling as loud as he could. The enemy's battery turned the guns on us as soon as they saw us coming, but we were moving so rapidly toward them that the shells passed over our heads. It looked as if we were going into the very jaws of death, for the enemy seemed, as we got nearer to them, to be in considerable force on the hill. The road made a slight dip just before it began to ascend, and for a moment we were out of sight of the enemy. I anxiously rode ahead to see what we would run up against, and to my delight as I ascended the hill I saw the battery limbering up and the whole line breaking in confusion.

The boldness and strangeness of the movement demoralized them. I could see the long bottom before us filled with fugitives. I have seen a statement from one of the enemy's artillery officers that they fired back at us as they retreated, and I remember that they did fire several shots which passed over our heads. A squadron of cavalry on our left started toward us, and I looked back anxiously for our infantry support, but a shot or two well aimed sickened them and they joined their defeated comrades.

Now we had everything our own way; the poor, panic-stricken wretches were flying before us in easy range of our guns and relentlessly we poured the shot and shell into them. It was awful; it seemed cruel, but, as Sherman said, "War is hell," the truth of which saying they were experiencing. We had left all our tender feeling behind on the field covered with our dead and dying comrades.

If Imboden could have gotten in their rear not a man would have escaped, but high water prevented it.

We continued our deadly fire on them until they crossed the bridge and burned it behind them. We put in our deadliest shots as they were packing like frightened cattle across the bridge. This ended the fight on Sunday. Imboden's brigade alone had been fighting them all day Saturday and had captured nearly an entire regiment of cavalry that had crossed Luray Gap to get in our rear. Imboden knew they

SIR MOSES EZEKIEL.

OPPOSITE PAGE 120.

were coming and had some men hid in the mountain, who got in their rear as soon as they passed at the top, beating them at their own game.

Soon after the fight I met young Sandy Stuart, one of the Cadets. I remember well what a gallant-looking fellow he was. He was wringing wet and his hands and face were black with powder. They had muzzle loaders then and the men had to bite the cartridges before putting them in the gun. He said, "Lieutenant, the blot on the Institute has been wiped out today by the best blood of Virginia." I replied, "Sandy, I never knew that there was a blot on the Institute." "Yes," he said, "your boys tried to put a stigma on us this morning, calling us bomb-proof and wagon dogs." "Oh," I replied, "my boys were only joking; they were all proud of you."

I write this article in justice to Imboden's brigade and McClanahan's battery, that have seldom been mentioned in accounts that I have seen of the battle. Imboden's brigade was composed of the Sixty-second Virginia Mounted Infantry, commanded by Col. George H. Smith; Eighteenth Virginia Cavalry, commanded by Col. George W. Imboden, and the Twenty-third Virginia Cavalry, commanded by Col. Robert White; McNeil's Rangers, and McClanahan's Horse Artillery.

Dr. Carter Berkeley states that "General Breckinridge had as a reserve force at New Market the Cadets and a regiment of old men. Major Semple, a staff officer, reported to him that there were not enough veterans to cover the Yankee line. The Cadets had sent him a committee, asking to be allowed to go in the battle, but the General had decided to hold them in reserve or as a rear-guard. When he was told that there was a gap in the line of battle that must be filled, he said, 'Then put in the boys, and may God forgive me!' bowing his head on his horse's neck as he spoke. I got this from Major Semple himself."

NOTE.—General Breckinridge, then Confederate Secretary of War, told me in Richmond in January, 1865, that the charge of the Cadets at New Market was the most splendid sight which he had ever witnessed. He said that they got into the charge without his knowing it; that he had tried to keep them out of harm's way. He heard the army cheering, looked in that direction and saw the Virginia Military Institute Battalion, which he knew at once by the songs of the men and their trim appearance, sweeping across the field as if it was on dress parade, and it was then too late to save it.

He said it almost broke his heart to see the boys dropping and the gaps torn in their line by the terrible fire; but that the way they closed up and went up to the Yankee guns was the most glorious thing ever seen in war. The Virginia Military Institute Battalion was not composed entirely of Virginians, but included boys from almost every Southern State.

H. H. H.

Another instance that touches the high-water mark is that of two of the Virginia Cadets at the Battle of New Market. On the battlefield Lieut. Carter Berkeley was passing when he was attracted by the cries of a mere boy, who said, "Sir, do get me a doctor; my friend is wounded!" Lieutenant Berkeley, drawing near, saw a young fellow seated, with his companion's head on his breast. Drawing nearer, he found two boys, and the one who had been calling him for his friend was grievously wounded himself, but so absorbed was he in looking after his companion that he had not even remarked that he was wounded. Lieutenant Berkeley said, "My poor boy, your friend is dead, but I will get a doctor for you."

A VIRGINIAN.

It seems hardly necessary to further mention the Cadets of the Virginia Military Institute, their heroism has been so widely exploited. The letter I subjoin was written immediately after the war, from Staunton, Va., to a friend in Baltimore; and I shall give, besides, some accounts of boys who fought the battle mentioned.

"STAUNTON, VA., *May 10th*, 1866.

"Today Captain Shipp, from the Institute, passed through with a squad on his way to Port Republic to bring the bodies of the seven Cadets who died in the battle of the 15th of May, in which General Breckinridge defeated Sigel. None of the two hundred and fifty Cadets were over sixteen, many under fourteen. Fourteen of them were wounded, eight killed.

"Many not as large as Henry (eleven years old). As their comrades fell they did not waver, but closed up at the word of command just as if on parade. All honor to the little heroes! They will remain in Staunton Saturday and Sunday. We shall strew their bier with flowers, but greatest honor of all, General Lee will attend their interment and doubtless drop a tear upon the sacred spot where they are laid. The

Cadets are going to erect a monument to them at the Institute. They will be interred the fifteenth, the anniversary of the day alike fatal to them and their enemies, for they were more than victorious, defeating Sigel, who had 3,500 men, and capturing his guns. It is said that one of them, a son of Mr. Seddon (Secretary of War of the Confederate States), was so young that he was unable to carry his gun and that one of his father's servants carried it for him on the march. Hugh Fry, one of the boys, captured a great big German officer, who refused to surrender his sword to such a child, until the boy threatened to run him through with his bayonet. It is in connection with this battle that Mr. Lincoln is said to have made his famous remark, 'How could you expect that Dutchman [Sigel] to win a battle.''

SIR MOSES EZEKIEL, SCULPTOR, ROME

Moses Ezekiel was born in Richmond in 1847. He entered the Virginia Military Institute in 1862 and was in the Battle of New Market with the corps of Cadets, a sergeant in Company C. He, with a number of other now prominent men, was a member of the third class and they all were in the battle together: Thos. G. Hayes, Mayor of Baltimore, 1900-1904; Dr. Botting Barton, of the Johns Hopkins University; Hon. John A. Wise, of Virginia, now a distinguished lawyer of New York, who ran for Governor of Virginia, but was defeated by Gen. Fitz Hugh Lee; Thos. R. Clendinen, a prominent lawyer of Baltimore, and many others. After the

ALEXANDER H. H. STUART, JR.

OPPOSITE PAGE 124.

war Ezekiel returned to the V. M. I., and graduated in 1866. He then went to Rome to study art, and as a sculptor became famous. He was knighted by the King of Italy, and made a chevalier of the Legion of Honor. Several of his works adorn the Corcoran Art Gallery in Washington; and at the Peabody Institute, in Baltimore, there is an exquisite bust of "The Christ," of which the beauty, grandeur and agony of expression are marvellous. He executed and presented a statue to the V. M. I. of "Virginia Mourning Her Dead," in memory of the eight Cadets who were killed at New Market and are buried on the parade ground of the Institute. This monument was unveiled the 4th of July, 1902, and he sent the following telegram:

"ROMA, *June* 23, 1903.

"To V. M. I., Lexington, Virginia:

"Adsum atque illustris complexus limina porte et memor et fidus gratulor. EZEKIEL."

Translation of Cable Message—"I am with you, and embracing the threshold of your illustrious portals, mindful of the past and faithful, I send congratulations EZEKIEL."

ALEXANDER H. H. STUART, JR.

Alexander H. H. Stuart, Jr., was the son of Hon. Alex. Hugh Holmes Stuart and Frances Cornelia Baldwin, and was born in Staunton, Va., on May 14, 1846. His paternal grandfather, Archibald Stuart, was a soldier in the Revolutionary War, and a member of the Convention of Virginia which ratified the Constitution of the United States. His maternal grandfather, Gerard B. Baldwin, was a member of the Supreme Court of Appeals of Virginia, and his father was Secretary of the Department of the Interior during President Fillmore's administration. A. H. H. Stuart, Jr., served as a member of the Corps of Cadets in the Battle of New Market, and continued in the military service of the Confederate Government until the close of the war. He then entered the University of Virginia, where he distinguished himself for scholarship. During the second year at the University he contracted typhoid fever and died at his father's home in Staunton on July 6, 1867.

CARRINGTON TAYLOR

Carrington Taylor was the son of Edwin Mygatt Taylor and Jane Eleanor Kinney, and was born in Staunton, Va., on December 1, 1845, and died in Richmond, Va., on October 28, 1875. His maternal grandfather was William Kinney, a Virginia lawyer of note, and his great-grandfather was General Robert Porterfield, a distinguished soldier in General Washington's army of the Revolutionary War. Carrington Taylor entered the Virginia Military Institute and served as a member of the Corps of Cadets in the Battle of New Market in 1862. He was afterwards a civil engineer and died from disease contracted from exposure while engaged in his profession.

FRANCIS TALIAFERRO BROOKE

Francis Taliaferro Brooke was born in Staunton, Va., September 12, 1846. He enlisted in McClanahan's Battery February 24, 1864, and served gallantly at New Market and up to the surrender. In 1866 he entered the Virginia Military Institute and is now a resident of Staunton.

EDWARD CARRINGTON KINNEY

Edward Carrington Kinney was born in Staunton, Va., March 20, 1845. In 1862 he was with his brother, an officer in General Forrest's command. He joined that command, and was with it until December, 1863, when he was transferred to the Army of Northern Virginia and joined McClanahan's battery, where he served gallantly (one of the boys at New Market) up to the surrender at Appomattox.

AUGUSTA'S BATTLE

On the 15th of May, 1864, General Breckinridge signally defeated Sigel and his hirelings at New Market, Va., which for a short time relieved the devoted people of the Shenandoah Valley of the presence of the hated foe.

Over and over again had this beautiful Valley been robbed and plundered and horribly had its inhabitants suffered, but nothing could dampen their ardor and love for the cause for which their sons were so heroically battling. But the worst had yet to come, for Lincoln had selected a renegade Virginian to still further try their loyalty and patriotism. Bill Arp, the noble Georgian, who has so recently "passed over the river," said, "That when a Virginian fell, he fell farther and harder than any other man could." Hunter, the apostate, crossed the Potomac the latter part of May and immediately began his horrid work by burning the beautiful homes of his own and his wife's kindred, where both he and his wife had often been hospitably entertained. His intention was to destroy everything on his march, but fortunately he had some officers with him more humane than himself, who protested against destroying private dwellings. To satisfy them he agreed to burn only barns and mills. Hunter may have agreed to this, but history shows that he did not stick to his agreement, for he not only in many cases burned dwellings, but also hung old men, non-combatants, and allowed his men to insult women and commit other outrages on the defenseless people.

General Imboden was then in the Valley with a small force, consisting of the Eighteenth Regiment of Virginia Cavalry, commanded by his brother, Col. Geo. Imboden; the Twenty-third Cavalry, by Col. Robt. White; Davis's Maryland Battalion of Cavalry, which had with it a company of old men over fifty-five years of age, commanded by Capt. Henry Harnsberger, and a company of boys, commanded by Capt. Geo. Chrisman; McNeil's Rangers, and McClanahan's six-gun battery of horse artillery, commanded by Capt. J. H. McClanahan. The regiments were all very much depleted by Imboden having the gaps in the mountains leading into West Virginia to guard. One of his best regiments, the Sixty-second Virginia Mounted Infantry, had gone with General Breckinridge, after the Battle of New Market, to Richmond. So with this meagre force

CARRINGTON TAYLOR.

OPPOSITE PAGE 128.

all he could do was to fall back, fighting and retarding the progress of the enemy as much as possible, hoping to be reinforced.

He first met Hunter about Woodstock, on the Valley turn-pike, and it was not until the 4th of June that Hunter had succeeded in forcing his way as far as Mount Crawford, in Rockingham County. His movements were slow, for he took up more time burning and making war on helpless women, old men and children, than he did marching or fighting. General Early says in his report: "The scenes on Hunter's route were truly heart-rending; houses had been burned and helpless women and children left without shelter. The country had been stripped of provisions, and many families left without a morsel to eat. Furniture and bedding had been cut to pieces and old men and children robbed of all the clothing they had except what was on their backs. Ladies' trunks had been robbed and their dresses torn to pieces in mere wantonness."

About the same time Sheridan had left the right of Grant's army with orders to make a junction with Hunter at Lynchburg, to capture and destroy that city, and move down on Lee's rear. But he found Hampton and Fitz Lee at Trevilian's and was terribly routed, and Hunter at Lynchburg found a lion in his path, brave old Jubal Early, who hurled him back into the mountains of West Virginia defeated, demoralized, and disgraced.

One can hardly imagine the feelings of our little band, as they fell back before the hordes of robbers and fire-fiends. At night the sky was lighted up with burning houses, and all day refugees were pouring into our lines, rending our hearts with their tales of horror.

General Imboden determined to make a final stand on the south bank of North River, near Mount Crawford, hoping to meet reinforcement there, which he did under Gen. W. E. Jones, who took command. He had with him Vaughan's Tennessee Brigade (dismounted cavalry); Sixtieth Virginia, Forty-fifth and Thirty-sixth Infantry, also Forty-fifth Battalion, and two regiments, composed of old men and boys and convalescents from the hospital at Staunton and workmen in the shops; Capt. Opie's company of Augusta farmers; Bryan's battery, and a battery made up for the occasion by boys from Staunton, and Augusta County. We had a good, defensible position there, and anxiously hoped they would attack us, but were disappointed. Before morning our scouts reported that the enemy had decamped in the night toward Port Republic. At early dawn General Jones sent Major Sturgis Davis's battalion with Harnsberger's and Chrisman's companies in that direction, followed by Imboden with his two regiments of cavalry. Davis met the advance guard of the enemy at Mount Meridian, and he reported that his old men and boys behaved splendidly. The boys had their first baptism of fire. General Stahl with a brigade of cavalry drove them and Imboden's cavalry back toward Piedmont, a village on the New Hope road in Augusta County. By that time our whole force had gotten to that place. The writer commanded a section of McClanahan's battery, and was ordered by General Jones to go rapidly to the front and aid Imboden in holding the enemy in check until he could get his line of battle formed.

I shall never forget the scene as we passed through the village, our horses on the run, and our boys yelling enthusiastically as they always did when going to the front. My boys were inspired by the glory of battle, and when that feeling takes possession of men, all fear vanishes. Lord Wolseley, the great English General, says: "I have never experienced the same unalloyed and elevating satisfaction, or known again the joy I felt, as I ran for the enemy's stockade at the head of a small mob of soldiers, most of them boys like myself."

We all had that feeling that day, and were inspired by one still stronger, for behind us were our mothers, wives, sisters and sweethearts. "At home bright eyes were sparkling for us, and we would defend them to the last." There were some ladies standing in a porch, waving their handkerchiefs and cheering as we passed, as was usual with the noble women of the Valley, when they saw our men going into battle. One of them cried out, "Lieutenant, don't let your men make so much noise; they will scare all the Yankees away before you can get a shot at them!" We passed through the village a few hours later; the dear women were gone, and the house they had left was riddled with shot and shell and filled with dead and wounded soldiers.

We soon came up to Imboden, retiring before an overwhelming body of cavalry, supported by infantry and artillery, and beyond the hill on which we took our position the whole country looked blue, and behind them was the smoke of burning barns. Although we were far ahead of our main body, we felt fairly safe, as we had supporting us Captain Opie's company and his gallant men from Augusta.

We had hardly begun firing before a section of the enemy's horse artillery ran out and opened on us. They seemed to be excited and fired wildly, but my boys replied coolly and deliberately, and soon silenced them. I have it from one of Hunter's staff officers, with whom I visited the battlefield since the war, that we knocked them out completely in a short time. He said, "I then put twelve guns on you and made you leave." I replied, "Yes, Colonel, you did make it hot for us, but we did not leave until we had orders to do so."

General Jones by that time had formed his line of battle. His infantry on the left, resting on Middle River, with a section of Bryan's battery supporting them. On the right was his cavalry, including Vaughn's brigade, a section of Bryan's battery. A space of at least a quarter of a mile in the center was defended by the boy battery and two sections of McClanahan's battery. The rest of the artillery was with the cavalry. In reserve he held Colonel Harper's and General Harman's regiments of old men, boys, and convalescents.

The enemy made their attack on our left, and gallantly did we hold our position for hours, time and again repulsing the attacks. At last they had to give way, but not until they had been worn to a frazzle. and nearly if not entirely out of ammunition, and most of their officers and many of their men killed and wounded, including the gallant commander, Colonel Brown, who died on the field.

We were soon surrounded by our own flying men, and in sight of the Yankees. Our men began to give

FRANCIS T. BROOKE.

OPPOSITE PAGE 132.

way. Jones became desperate, rushed impetuously to the front, followed by many of Harper's men, right on to the Yankee line of battle, which poured a deadly volley into them, killing Jones and many others. Just then Col. Robt. Doyle, who with other officers was trying to rally our men, was also killed. I had just gotten my guns unlimbered and would have fired but was peremptorily ordered by a staff officer of the dead general to limber up and try to save my guns. I would have lost them I believe had I stayed a minute longer. My boys were behaving splendidly and would have stood by the guns until the last.

In our retreat, we had to pass through a piece of woods, and my intention was to make a stand as soon as I got out of the woods. Flying men were all around us and a regiment of Yankee cavalry right behind us. This cavalry had been pushed to the front to take advantage of the break in our line and complete the victory now nearly won. As we got out of the woods I saw a section of McClanahan's battery, commanded by Lieut. Park Collett, standing in the road limbered up and evidently oblivious of the critical condition of things. I called out to him to get into battery, that the Yankees were right behind us, intending to unlimber my section as soon as I got in line with him, but it was too late, for before we had time to get into battery the enemy burst out of the woods with yells of triumph, sabring, shooting, and riding down our poor fellows. But it was the last yell that some of them ever gave, for just in front of them were McClanahan's guns and behind the guns were men who had never been run off a battlefield. By the time I got to him Collett had unlimbered and shotted his guns, and the gunners were standing with the lanyards in their hands, hesitating to fire; and when I called out to them to do so, one of them said, "Lieutenant, we will kill our own men." There was no time to lose; they would have been over us in a minute more; so I jumped off my horse and made a grab for the lanyard in the hands of the gunner nearest me; but he anticipated me and pulled it off himself, the other gunners doing the same, and I never before saw two shots do such execution. The whole head of the Yankee column seemed to melt away. The timely and gallant action of Collett saved everything, all of our guns and wagons. The men who were not captured retreated on the Mount Sidney road. The officer who commanded the advance of the Yankee column was in Staunton some years ago, and said that the two companies in advance, as they came out of the woods, were never organized again.

It is sweet to die for one's country, to fall with your breast bared to the deadly storm in the defense of truth and justice and for loved ones. But is there any glory to die in the act of shooting down and sabring old men and boys who are trying to prevent their country from being robbed and plundered, and their women from being insulted?

Soon after Collett began firing, General Imboden came up and said, "You are doing the right thing. How long can you hold this position?" The reply was, "We have stopped here for good." He said that the Eighteenth Regiment was coming to our support. Soon it came, and it was suggested to the General to charge down the road that we might redeem the day; but he only threw out a line of battle and we held the position.

I had been in a good many battles, but this was the first time my command was driven off the field, and now it fills my heart with indignation to know that there are men who wore the gray, who for the sake of an office are base enough to go North and tell the people who robbed and humiliated us that they are glad of it; that it was best for us to have lost. No doubt they weep when they read how gallant old Jubal Early defeated Hunter at Lynchburg.

This was Augusta's battle, and on the bloody field old men and boys laid down their lives in the vain attempt to save their people from Hunter's barn-burners. Is it any reason that because they failed we should not raise a monument to keep their memories green in the hearts of their posterity? Ought not their names at least to be put on record in the archives of the county? I appeal to Augusta's noble women to see that justice is done to these heroes.

This is a very inaccurate account of the battle, I know; but there was never an official report of it made. I had no data to guide me, and I had to depend on my memory. I would like to have had the list of Augusta's killed and wounded and I would be obliged to any one who will furnish me the names, for they ought certainly to be put on record in the archives of the county.

A section of Bryan's battery was commanded by Sergt. Milton W. Humphreys and did splendid service on the left. Prof. Humphreys is professor of Greek at the University of Virginia. Major Saunders, of the Forty-fifth Regiment, was left for dead on the field, but was revived and saved by Mrs. Crawford, who lived near the battlefield.

I have been told since by Col. George Imboden, who commanded on the extreme right, that most of Stahl's cavalry was immediately in his front and ready to run around our right wing if he had moved away. He said that General Jones had told General Imboden in the morning that he must hold the right, or Hunter would cut us off from Waynesboro, our base.

CARTER BERKELEY.

WILLIAM T. WHEATLEY

William T. Wheatley was born in Charles County on March 20, 1844, about three miles from the village of Waldorf. When the Civil War broke out he was fifteen years of age. He then went to Richmond, Va., where he joined Company I of the First Maryland Regiment, Capt. Michael S. Robertson. This was the famous Bucktail Regiment. In the second year of the war he joined the Second Maryland Battalion, becoming a member of Company B, with Capt. J. Parran Crane, now Judge Crane, of Maryland.

This youthful soldier went through the whole war and took part in such history-making battles as Front Royal, Cross Keys and Gettysburg, besides a number of smaller engagements. He was wounded twice, once at Gettysburg. He was also captured twice. The first time was at Hatch's Run. After a short time he was exchanged, with 5,000 other sick and disabled soldiers, and reported for duty within twenty days. His second capture was in front of

UNIVERSITY OF VIRGINIA

OPPOSITE PAGE 136.

Richmond, when Grant made his onslaught upon the Confederate Capital. This was on April 3, 1865, and on June 21 he was paroled and returned home.

In July of that year he came to Baltimore and took a place as clerk in the firm of Wheatley & Anderson, of which his uncle, J. Frank Wheatley, was a member. This firm went out of business two years later, and, through his uncle's recommendation, he was given the then unimportant place of secretary of the Corn and Flour Exchange. His subsequent history has been very much in the public eye, and the affectionate regard which his associates entertain for him is exemplified by the action taken in 1892, when a magnificent silver service was presented to him in honor of the twenty-fifth year of his incumbency of the office of secretary.

BILLINGS STEELE

Billings Steele, one of Mosby's lieutenants, died suddenly of pneumonia on Sunday night at the residence of his sister, Mrs. A. W. Habersham, in Annapolis, Md.

Mr. Steele was a bachelor, in his fifty-third year. He was the youngest son of Henry Maynadier Steele and Maria Lloyd Key, of Tollys, near Annapolis. He was a nephew of the late I. Nevett Steele, of Baltimore, and a grandson of Francis Scott Key, author of the "Star-Spangled Banner."

On the breaking out of the war, although but sixteen years of age, he, in company with his brother, Frank Key Steele, at once crossed the Potomac. Their intention was to join the Regular Army, but

Billings, being a fine horseman, concluded to cast his lot with Mosby's guerrillas, which he did, and served with bravery and distinction until the close. He won his promotion in the famous greenback raid.

ROBERT M'KIM

Robert McKim was born in Baltimore on December 24, 1843, and was therefore a little over eighteen years of age when he fell at the battle near Winchester, Va., on May 25, 1862.

His fate was one of those sad incidents of our Civil War which are most painful to recall. How little availed the great sacrifices made by those gallant, noble spirits who fought for principles and honor! And yet the short life of this young man was full of grace and beauty. His varied and admirable intellectual gifts and his charming personal traits so endeared him to those who knew him that they cannot cease to cherish his memory and mourn his early death.

In the autumn of 1860, when only sixteen years old, he entered the University of Virginia. Those were stirring times; and the students were much excited by the rumors of war and the troubles that crowded thick and fast over our country. Much of their time was spent in military training, and the burning questions of the day superseded all other interests. During the few months that Robert spent at the University his character developed rapidly. He possessed great personal beauty, and a charming tenor voice made him a favorite amongst his fellow-students.

This beautiful voice is even to-day recalled by his friends and comrades with the greatest pleasure. At every reunion of his old comrades and fellow-soldiers, the old songs, sung over the camp-fires, after days of trial, hard fighting and forced marches, are recalled with touching remembrance of that bright young life.

In a scrap-book which came to the family after the war were several letters and mementos from his college friends. They always called him "Honest Bob," and allusions were made to the brightest and happiest associations. And yet his letters home were full of earnest thoughts and high aspirations, and he proved himself, during his college and army life, an earnest Christian and sincerely religious.

When the University was closed in June, 1861, Robert, with his cousin, Randolph McKim, and others, started for Maryland. At Winchester they were detained, waiting for passes to cross the lines. They were there when the Confederate Army passed through, on its way to Manassas. Ardent and enthusiastic, and fully persuaded that the cause of the South was a righteous one, these young men enlisted then and there. Robert joined the artillery,—the Rockbridge Battery,—commanded by General Pendleton, which formed part of the famous Stonewall Jackson's Brigade. A few days afterwards the great Battle of Bull Run was fought. What an experience for a boy only seventeen, with little military training, and no possible knowledge of the horrors of war! From that time he continued a member of the Stonewall Brigade; enduring the greatest hardships, entailed by forced marches, with insufficient clothing, no tents and little food. The heroism of that campaign will never be fully appreciated; and yet his letters, written at this time, told of the brightest hopes, and the descriptions of their life and adventures were full of wit and humor. In them he spoke of the Maryland soldiers as suffering terribly, but being at the same time the merriest fellows in the army, and the best marchers. He said: "Oh, how I long for the spring to come, when we will cross the river and take Washington, and then march in triumph to dear old Baltimore!" Alas, in the spring he did indeed cross the river. On May 23, 1862, General Jackson began the march down the Luray Valley. The Stonewall Brigade had several encounters with the Federal forces, and succeeded in driving General Banks back toward Winchester. The Marylanders were much exhilarated, and looked forward to crossing into Maryland as a certainty. The night before the 25th the fighting was very severe and the first division of the Rockbridge Artillery was in action continually. Early on that morning the Confederates advanced, and during a severe fight, about six o'clock, Robert was killed—struck by the ball of a sharp-shooter. Through the kindness of loving friends he was carried into Winchester, and buried there, temporarily. He was later brought to Baltimore and buried in the family vault at Greenmount.

One of his old friends, in writing to the family lately, said: "About Bob McKim I have but one recollection; and that is the pleasure his company always gave me. He was a gallant boy, always bright and cheerful, and never complaining of any lot. It was just such material as he furnished that gave the Confederate soldier his undying reputation."

WILLIAM JANNEY HULL.

OPPOSITE PAGE 140.

(By Father Ryan.)

"Young as the youngest who donned the Gray,
True as the truest that wore it,
Brave as the bravest—he marched away—
(Hot tears on the cheeks of his mother lay);
Triumphant waved our flag one day,
He fell in the front before it.

"Firm as the firmest where duty led,
He hurried without a falter;
Bold as the boldest he fought and bled,
And the day was won—but the field was red—
And the blood of his fresh young heart was shed
On his country's hallow'd altar.

"On the trampled breast of the battle plain,
Where the foremost ranks had wrestled,
On his pale pure face—not a mark of pain—
(His mother dreams they will meet again)
The fairest form amid all the slain,
Like a child asleep he nestled."

EMILIE MCKIM REED.

WILLIAM JANNEY HULL

William Janney Hull was a member of the Fifty-third Maryland Regiment, and when he was eighteen it was called out by a general alarm to defend Baltimore against the Pennsylvania mob, marching on the town to sack it in revenge for the 19th of April. There is nothing more terrifying than the alarm bell at night, and I never shall forget as he prepared to go, how young and boyish he looked putting on his uniform, as gaily as if for a dance. Immediately after this he went South, but of course could not wear his uniform. The Adams Express was still running, and it was one of their rules to forward party finery "with haste," so I wrote on the box I sent containing the uniform, "For a ball," and it reached him "with haste" and safely. Events justified the play on words. He entered the Confederate service, and did his duty faithfully until the surrender. He was with General Imboden under General Early in his campaign in the Valley of Virgina, and was wounded near Lynchburg. I drove over the road they followed in pursuing Averell in his raid. My cousin, Judge J. Thompson Brown, also one of the pursuers, was with me and told me that the small streams we were then fording so easily at the time of the raid were over their banks and frozen slush extended for many hundred yards. The ice in the soldiers' boots had to be thawed before they could be removed.

CHARLES WYNDHAM GAY

Charles W. Gay was the idol and pride of his family, and his love for his mother and sisters seemed to be a talisman to keep him unspotted from the world. He was a great student, but the day Virginia cast in her lot with the sister States he resolved to volunteer as a private soldier. His health was frail and his friends urged him to seek some less exposed position, but the front of the battle was his choice and in order to fit himself for the service he went with his younger brother, Erskine, only sixteen, to Lexington to study the elements of military tactics. They both enlisted July 1, 1861, in the University Volunteers, and Charles soon gained the rank of sergeant. The Volunteers were disbanded in the fall and the following spring Charles and Erskine set out from Staunton to join the Army of the Shenandoah. After a long and fatiguing march they came up with it a few miles from Strasburg, and without stopping for food or rest immediately joined the Rockbridge Artillery, and in an hour or two were taking part in the Battle of Kernstown, in which the Rockbridge Battery did memorable service. This battery was part of the Stonewall Brigade, and nearly every section of the South and all the professions were represented on its rolls—*eight* students of Divinity in Charles's mess alone. Later the Gay brothers joined the Danville Artillery, under Captain Wooding, Third Brigade of Jackson's division, and did gallant service in nearly every engagement of the brilliant campaign of 1862. Charles's glowing descriptions of his sensations as they charged the routed columns of Banks through the streets of Winchester amid wild cheers of welcome show how completely the student was merged in the daring, enthusiastic young soldier. The Danville Artillery was now ordered before Richmond, threatened by McClellan, and through all the heavy fighting that followed occupied advanced positions on the line. For six long bloody days the battle raged with unabated fury. Charles never left his post, his young brother always near him; nor did his brave spirit falter. He was very ill, really unfit for duty, but he calmly stood to his gun, by his example inspiring his comrades with equal courage. On the memorable day of Malvern Hill the battery got into position under a heavy fire from the gunboats on the James, and as his piece was brought into line a fragment of a shell struck him in the shoulder and neck, causing instant death. His body was borne from the field by his brother Erskine and received a soldier's burial in a neighboring churchyard. Later it was removed to Hollywood, there to await the last great reveille. So lived and died this young soldier, leaving to us the memory of a blameless life and a heroic death, and a sincere belief that for him it was but a step from the clash of arms to a realm of perfect peace.

ERSKINE GAY

Erskine Gay enlisted in the University Volunteers with his brother Charles, and their lives in the Army ran side by side until the terrible morning when Erskine carried the body of his beloved brother off the field of battle, returning instantly to his post of duty, with what agony the Reader of all hearts alone knows, as his brother's name has never passed his lips in all these years. He nobly and faithfully served his country until the surrender, with Stonewall Jackson's gallant band of heroes—and is now living on the family estate, Gaymont, near Staunton, and is Commander of the Stonewall Jackson Camp of Volunteers.

RANDOLPH HARRISON M'KIM

Randolph Harrison McKim, of Baltimore, was a boy of nineteen at the University of Virginia when the war broke out, and immediately joined a company of University Volunteers, and marched to Harper's Ferry. He fought with this company until the Maryland regiments were organized, when he was transferred to the Second Maryland Infantry in Cap-

RANDOLPH HARRISON M'KIM.

OPPOSITE PAGE 144.

tain William Murray's company, under Gen. Geo. Steuart, on whose staff he was afterwards appointed. He had many narrow escapes, his horse being shot under him frequently. The most remarkable was at the Battle of Gettysburg. At Culp's Hill the ammunition ran out and supplies could only be obtained by the men passing under a terrible fire of the enemy. General Steuart called for volunteers for the desperate attempt. Young McKim said, "General, do not call for volunteers while you have a staff officer left;" and taking four men, he brought the needed ammunition in blankets, literally *walking* "the gauntlet," as so heavily laden rapid motion was impossible. Strange to say they passed unscathed—let us hope through the recognition by their foes of such dauntless sustained courage. Young McKim fought gallantly until the close of the war and then entered the ministry, as he always intended. There are some interesting letters in possession of his family telling of the serious religious tone of his regiment, and of the prayer meetings in camp, of which he was a leader. The fact of so many divinity students and even ordained ministers taking active part in the struggle shows that the principles for which they fought were not incompatible with devotion to God and His service.

"My men are out of ammunition, sir," said Capt. William Murray. "I will bring the ammunition, if I live."

Words that should be written in letters of gold, and they fell from the lips of Lieut. Randolph McKim.

COMPANY A, SECOND MARYLAND INFANTRY

Company A, Second Maryland, was composed almost entirely of very young men and boys, some of them members of Company H, First Maryland Infantry. In battle they not only showed heroic courage in attack, but were dauntless, unwavering, exalted in defeat. At Culp's Hill, at the Battle of Gettysburg, after such an unparalleled charge that it has immortalized them, "of 900 brave men against the bayonets of 10,000 foemen and artillery innumerable," *up* the side of a mountain, the enemy entrenched behind line above line of fortifications, they were almost destroyed and were compelled to retreat. But it was no rout, no disorganized flight. The men moved down the mountain as if on parade, their officers marching backwards, faces to the foe, marking time with their swords. I shall tell of some of the brave boys who either took part in this charge or lay dead or wounded on the field.

WILLIAM HOLLINS BOWLY

William Hollins Bowly was the first boy over the fortifications at Culp's Hill. As the regiment reformed the enemy discharged a volley and he was instantly killed—only nineteen years old in the fourth year of the war.

LAMAR HOLLYDAY

Lamar Hollyday, in the last charge on Culp's Hill, was wounded in the thigh in his effort to reach a

RANDOLPH HARRISON M'KIM.

OPPOSITE PAGE 146.

Union color-bearer just before the retreat began. After he fell he was shot a second time, and a huge Yankee, seizing him by the arm, dragged him some distance, his shattered leg in agony. When they reached the breastworks some one asked, "Isn't that a Rebel?" And he called out sturdily, "Yes, I *am* a Rebel!"

CHARLES L. BRADDOCK

Charles L. Braddock was so young that he ran away and went into the Army without the consent of his mother. At the Battle of Gettysburg, when his company was charging the enemy at Culp's Hill, he exclaimed, "Do you call this war? I call it fun!" Later he was seen fighting before Petersburg, but after that nothing was ever heard of him, though his mother watched and waited for news of her boy.

CHARLES TILGHMAN LLOYD

Charles Tilghman Lloyd was carried off the battlefield of Gettysburg wounded, but returned to his post almost immediately, to be wounded a second time—this time mortally.

SOMERVILLE PINKNEY GILL

Somerville Pinkney Gill was killed instantly, after passing through this baptism of fire, at the Battle of Peeble's Farm, aged twenty-one, in the fourth year of the war. His body was never found.

DR. TALMAGE'S STORY

In assisting to capture the rifle-pits on the Squirrel Level road, Willis G. D. Baxley, aged seventeen, was mortally wounded, at the same time with William Scholley Prentiss. Dr. Talmage was visiting the hospital in Washington and a bright young fellow called him and said: "Doctor, I want to tell you something. You think I am one of your people; I am not, I'm a Rebel." The Doctor set his mind at rest and told him it did not make the slightest difference. Prentiss was again wounded at Petersburg, and on being taken to the hospital of the Sixth Army Corps he met his brother, Major Prentiss, of the Union Army—also severely wounded. The two brothers died there together!

SAMUEL BOWYER DAVIS

Samuel Bowyer Davis was wounded at Gettysburg, and taken prisoner to Chester; but by bribing his guard made his escape. On his way South, at Easton, he met Otho Williams on the boat with several Federal officers. Mr. Williams said, "How do you do, Davis. I thought you were in Virginia." Davis answered, "You are mistaken, sir; that is not my name." Finally he reached Richmond and was sent to Andersonville, in charge of Union prisoners; but later meeting a friend who had been ordered on very dangerous duty, he volunteered to take his place. This was to take dispatches to Canada in regard to John Yates Beall. Davis reached Canada safely, but was captured in Indiana on his return, and being recognized by a former prisoner at Andersonville was condemned to death as a spy. The morning he was to be hung the jailer said, "Davis, we have your cravat ready for you." He answered, "I will show you how a Southern man can die for his country." He was reprieved, however, by order of President Lincoln, through the influence of Mrs. Turnbull, and sentenced to imprisonment for life in Albany. He was pardoned in 1865. His speech in his own defense was said to have been worthy of Demosthenes.

PARKER'S BOY BATTERY

Dr. Hale says: "The Battle of Gettysburg was won by boys whose ages averaged twenty-three." We call those *men*. On the Southern side battles were lost or won by boys averaging sixteen years old, real school boys; with young officers of high rank from seventeen to twenty-four—so nobly fought that Gen. S. D. Lee, addressing Parker's Boy Battery after an engagement in which they had distinguished themselves, said, "You are boys, but you have gone this day where only men could go." The retreat from Gettysburg was covered at one point by two guns of that battery, which remained in position some time after the retreat had begun. A Confederate officer rode up to Captain Parker and demanded why he did not go. He replied he had no order from competent authority to do so. Receiving this order, that little battery retired, slowly following the regiments which were leaving the field in good order, their officers walking backwards step by step, face to foe. History presents no other such picture. A

United States officer stated afterwards that his force was prevented from pursuing and attacking the retreating army by this battery, as no one would have supposed it could have been left in that position without strong support.

"STAUNTON, *November* 13, 1904.

"MY DEAR COUSIN:

"The children received your note about war recollections, but in this busy day, that time is seldom in mind; and I have never interested myself much in the renaissance of Confederate ideas forty years after the facts. It reminds me of the small boys prancing around on the saw dust with their stick horses after the circus has left town. I was first in the Botts Grays, Second Infantry, in the taking of the arsenal at Harper's Ferry, the first "event" in Virginia. My brother Briscoe was with us, not quite fifteen. At Brandy Station he got several sabre wounds, and was a prisoner at Old Capitol. Afterwards I was the youngest officer in the Fifty-second Infantry, and the youngest man except one—our little blind drummer, Maurice. When Milroy attacked our camp on the Alleghany, at dawn of December 13, I pulled Maurice out of his bunk and made him beat the long roll down the street of the camp, *before making his toilet,* and I can almost hear him swearing yet. He was not quite fourteen. It was very cold, but got warmer in a few minutes. At First Manassas, when Jackson's line, broken by the charge of the New York Zouaves, reformed and took the guns of the Rhode Island Battery, the nearest one killed to the cannon was a fair-haired boy in V. M. I. Cadet uniform, hardly fourteen, who

THOMAS D. RANSON.

OPPOSITE PAGE 150.

was shot through the heart as he jumped over a little brush fence almost in reach of the gunners; and I shall never forget how brave and handsome he looked with his little dress sword clinched in his hand. Baylor's Light Horse, from Jefferson County, was made up almost altogether of boys at first, and their dash and gallantry was the talk of the whole cavalry command. I hardly ever saw a fight without seeing boys at the front.

"Your affectionate cousin,

"THOS. D. RANSON."

THOMAS D. RANSON

One of General Stuart's special detail of scouts, operating for the department of Secret Service on the B. and O. R. R. in the lower Valley, took it into his head to go home to see—a sister. His home was Charlestown, a historic village, changing hands between Federals and Confederates many times in a day, but never its principles and sympathies. It was "blue" enough at this time, a brigade of infantry in undisturbed but vigilant possession. The visitor had to leave old "Stockinglegs" and do some traveling on all fours to reach cover of his roof-tree, and unfortunately having stirred up the pickets was not only cut off from his horse but unable for two days and nights either to get away or to see that "sister," except an exasperating view through the cracks in the shutters of an unsuccessful interview between her and a "corporal of the guard." It was the day of hoopskirts, and the lady in the case had under that sanction an elegant pair of cavalry boots, the latest New York and Washington papers, and letters galore for the boys in camp. She finally flanked that picket and got through at another point. She was postmistress for Company B, but not by Federal appointment. He crawled out that night between the pickets, and faithful Old John, one of a dozen negroes, big and little, who had been helping to hide him, and lying to the Yankees, and who would have died sooner than betray him, brought him a little Canadian pony that had been hidden in a cellar, and he made his way to Harper's Ferry. There a friend, a citizen, met him with more Northern newspapers. While they were talking, such long trains began passing the Ferry in such quick succession from the West, without stopping, that their curiosity was aroused. A dozen trains loaded with troops and artillery were explanation enough to the scout of a sudden movement of the Army of the West, withdrawn from Bragg's front, to reinforce Meade for an assault upon the unprepared troops of Lee in their scattered winter quarters. It was not very long before that pony was twenty miles away, swimming the Shenandoah, swollen by heavy rains. Horse and rider were carried by the current far below the ford, and landed drenched and exhausted. Yet that little Canadian pony held out for some twenty miles more with one hurried feed, then sank down and died while the saddle was being buckled on a fresh steed impressed from a farmer by the roadside. Somehow, like a nightmare ride, the eighty-five miles or more were covered, report made to General Stuart, the scout sent on without a moment's delay to General Lee, and almost as quickly admitted to his tent, the simple headquarters of the

Army of Northern Virginia. There he was received with as much politeness as if the boy private was a corps commander, and in less than ten minutes the General knew all that was in him and had left the tent. What followed was a blank for perhaps two hours, the last words heard being orders quietly and rapidly given for the movement and concentration of the troops. He waked as he had waked more than once on that uncanny ride, with a feeling that the next step would carry his horse over an awful precipice. He had been broken down from loss of sleep at the start, and the ride had almost finished him. The torture had been indescribable. All the phantasms and vagaries imaginable attended it. Men cantering alongside and in front of him were ghosts to the touch; river and forest and mountains blended confusedly, but the powerful will controlled the body and it acted mechanically. Before he could realize where he was, the tent fly was softly opened and General Lee's noble face appeared. Seeing his guest awake he entered. It seems that the tired boy had fallen forward from the camp chair to the General's cot, in a dead sleep, the moment he had been left. General Lee, returning, had thrown a cloak over him, left him in possession, tied the tapes of the tent door, and actually stood guard before it in the bleak winter night, that the boy might sleep uninterrupted as the couriers came and went. To say the boy was ashamed would poorly express his feelings, but it was even more embarrassing to have a special supper served to him in the General's tent and to be honored by compliments on what he had done. The supper was the same he saw several times later served at the General's mess, and just what was issued to his men in the ranks; but the scanty ration was garnished with the grace of his courtesy and dignity. Is it any wonder that his men loved "Marse Bob?" What other commander, at such a time, would have shown such delicate consideration for a soldier boy? Sure enough the purpose was a sudden attack on Lee, but Meade's blow was not delivered. His stealthy advance found Lee waiting in strong entrenchments, ready and willing for a fight, so Meade went to entrenching on his own account. He is said to have declared that he could carry the position with the loss of thirty thousand men, but as that idea was so frightful there seemed nothing to do but retire, so at the end of four days he backed out and retreated to the Rapidan.

HENRY ALBERT ROBY

Henry Albert Roby, of Baltimore, wished to run the blockade and join the Southern Army, but could not leave without saying farewell to his mother, and hesitated, fearing she would not consent to his fighting in the Confederate ranks. However, she made no objection, like many another "Spartan" mother, only asking him to wait until he was eighteen—possibly hoping his ardor would cool by that time. But one terrible night, a short time after his eighteenth birthday, the rain pouring in torrents, he knelt to receive her parting blessing, and went out into the storm to make his way across the lines. He reached Harry Gilmor's command safely, but after a short time was attached to the First Mary-

GENERAL LEE AS PRESIDENT OF WASHINGTON COLLEGE.

OPPOSITE PAGE 154.

land Battalion, under Captain Dement. At the Battle of Gettysburg his caisson was separated from the gun to which it belonged, and in order to supply the gun with ammunition he had again and again to run the gauntlet of a terrific fire. He was much complimented by his superior officer for his courage and endurance in such a dangerous position. This caisson was afterwards struck by a shell and he was thrown into the air by the force of the explosion. In falling he struck one of the wheels, but strange to say was not seriously injured, but fought nobly and gallantly until the end of the war. At the time of the war with Spain he wrote this little poem calling on the brothers in Blue and Gray—an instance of what President Davis said, that "A brave man cannot hate."

BLUE AND GRAY

"Hear the Nation's bugle-call,
Blue and Gray;
Up and rally one and all,
Blue and Gray!
Sons of sires who fought with Lee,
With Grant, so great in victory,
Unite to day!

"Hark the cannon's thunder call,
Blue and Gray;
Let once more a new Stonewall,
Blue and Gray,
Front the 'Blood and gold of Spain'
Flaunting o'er the murdered Maine
In Havana's bay!

"Not against a brother's breast,
Blue and Gray;
Shall the bayonet be pressed
In this fray.
Let the cruel foreign foe
Gloat o'er bleeding Cuba's woe
While they may.—

"Gathering in resistless might,
Blue and Gray;
Armed by justice for the fight,
Blue and Gray;
Now for freedom draw the sword,
Trust for victory to the Lord—
Forward! Blue and Gray!"

THOMAS JACKSON WATERS

Thomas Jackson Waters, of St. Mary's County, Md., in his eighteenth year joined the First Virginia Cavalry, under Captain George R. Gaither, one of Maryland's bravest sons. In the retreat from Gettysburg he was captured and taken first to Capitol Prison and later to Point Lookout in his own county. There one morning he heard two prisoners discussing a plan of escape, and asking how it was to be done, G. M. Surpell, of Prince George's County, told him they were going to try to get away that night by swimming the river. Young Waters said that would do him no good as he could not swim a stroke; but the other prisoner, Mulay, of Texas, said, "Never mind, come along; we'll get away somehow." So that night, a little before eight o'clock, when the guard's back was turned, not more than ten feet away, the three men bolted, ran to the river, and hid behind the cliff, and though sought for diligently were not found. As soon as it was very dark they crawled along the beach until they came to some planks, on which they pushed out into the water. About half a mile from shore, his two companions crying, "Well, good-by, Waters, every man for himself!" swam off and he was alone on a plank in the middle of the Potomac River, not able to swim. He hung on as best he could, however, and paddled along until nearly sunrise, when, half dead with exhaustion, he was washed ashore near St. Jerome's Creek, eight miles from where they struck out. They must all have been carried by the current to about the same place, as after walking along the bank a little while he met both of his companions. They hid in the woods all day, meeting an old farmer named Richardson, who gave them food, and as soon as night fell assisted them to get away. They passed through Washington safely and eventually reached their commands. Young Waters was near the gallant J. E. B. Stuart when he was killed at Yellow Tavern, and helped to lift him off his horse. He fought bravely until the surrender, in the Wilderness, in sixty battles in sixty days, and even afterwards, whenever the slightest criticism was made on the South and its heroes.

JOHN EMORY SUDLER

John Emory Sudler left home in February, 1862, to join the Confederate cavalry with his chum, Thomas H. Gemmill, who had already enlisted in the First Maryland Cavalry at Richmond, and had returned home to raise funds to help equip the regiment, as the Southern cavalrymen had to furnish their own horses. Young Sudler wanted to take his favorite horse with him, but it was impossible, and he sold "Moloch" in Baltimore—a sad beginning to the young fellow's career, to part with so true and dear a friend as a future cavalryman's favorite horse must be. The two friends journeyed warily through lower Maryland, finally reaching Chaptico, where they waited in hiding for a favorable night to cross—joined by two Confederate officers, Captain Ward, on General Trimble's staff, and Mr. Williams, and some young traders with contraband goods. The night came, one to delight the heart of a blockade-runner, the wind blowing furiously, a heavy snow falling. The boat, commanded by Captain Cawood, an experienced blockader, was rowed by six stalwart negroes, with muffled oars, and orders given in whispers. Just at the start a young man came up and said his name was Bowie and he must get to Virginia that night, so he was hustled aboard and the boat put off. Half way across, at a hurried signal, the men stopped rowing, and not a minute too soon, as a gunboat passed so close the man in the bow could have touched it with his oar. They were all rejoicing at the danger past, when "Bowie" sprang up, and before he could be prevented fired two shots from his revolver after the retreating gunboat. Its engines were stopped, but fortunately she could not tell from what direction the shots came, and while she was moving first north, then south, then north again, the rowboat, carrying no light, was making rapid progress toward the Virginia shore. At dawn the gunboat discovered the whereabouts of the rowboat, and shot and shell began whistling through the air; but the boat touching bottom in about a foot of water, no order was ever more instantly obeyed than that of Captain Cawood's, "Get ashore!" The young traders, unwilling to leave their goods, were captured. "Bowie" disappeared. Was he "Bowie" or a Yankee spy?

Young Sudler reached Harry Gilmor's command in safety and was made captain of the Second Maryland Cavalry, and served gallantly until the surrender at Appomattox. He was wounded in the ankle at Chancellorsville and received a sabre cut at the Battle of Cedar Creek.

The following constitute a little group of schoolmates of John Emory Sudler, who lost their lives in the Confederate Army—all from Kent County, Md.:

John Chapman Spencer, son of Samuel W. Spencer, cashier of the State Bank at Chestertown, at about seventeen years of age enlisted in the First Maryland Cavalry, and was killed at Greenbrier Gap, W. Va., in 1863.

Thomas H. Gemmill, son of Dr. Wm. H. Gemmill, of Kent County, enlisted in the First Maryland Cavalry and was killed in a charge near Winchester in 1863.

Levi Perkins, son of Mr. Isaac Perkins, of Kent County, enlisted in the First Maryland Cavalry, and was killed at Sandy Spring, Maryland, in 1864.

Harvey Blackistone, son of Wm. H. Blackistone, of Kent County, was lieutenant in First Maryland Cavalry, and was killed in a fight at Bunkers Hill, near Winchester, in 1864.

Alfred Kennard, son of Dr. Kennard, of Kent County, enlisted in the Western Army under Albert Sidney Johnston, and was killed at Shiloh in 1862.

Benjamin C. Vickers, son of the Hon. George Vickers, of Kent County, enlisted in McCullough's Texas Rangers, and was killed in 1862.

JOHN THOMPSON MASON

John Thompson Mason was a son of Major Isaac S. Rowland, a volunteer officer in the Mexican War, and Cathrine Armstead Mason, of Loudoun County, Va. He was born in 1844. His father died when he was only five years old, and his maternal grandfather, John Thompson Mason, of Virginia, having no son of his own and wishing to perpetuate the distinguished name of Mason, requested that this child should take the name, which was done by act of court. Just before the war he received the promise of an appointment to the Naval Academy from Mr. Lovejoy, the famous abolitionist, through the influence of Mr. Brownson Murray and his aunt, Miss Emily V. Mason. Having to reside in the State from which he was appointed, he went to Illinois after spending his last Christmas (as it proved) in the Fairfax County home, "The Cottage," the Christmas of 1860. At his home so near Washington the political excitement raised the winter temperature to fever heat. As early as January, 1861, secession cockades were made and worn in Virginia, of the Virginia colors—blue and gold—the button bearing the Virginia coat of arms. One of these was sent to Mason, and the boy, in a spirit of mischief, wore it pinned to his jacket. Lovejoy heard of it and sent the following letter to Miss Mason, which is preserved among her papers. The irate abolitionist writes:

"WASHINGTON, *February* 1, 1861.

"I have learned that your boy has been sporting a dis-union badge since he left. This, of course, settles the question of his nomination. To avoid all discussion or importunity I have taken steps to give it to another,"

JOHN THOMPSON MASON.

OPPOSITE PAGE 160.

Jack was at home when Virginia seceded and was eager to enter the Virginia army. He was only fourteen years of age. Too young to enlist, he was received as a "marker" in the Alexandria County Seventeenth Virginia Infantry, and was in the First Battle of Manassas, and in the trenches all night in the rain and mud after the first day's battle. When he walked in to see his mother, who was in Fauquier County, he was so black from dirt and powder that she did not know him.

Shortly after the Battle of Manassas, Mason was appointed midshipman in the Confederate Navy and sent to the naval school ship *Patrick Henry*. He served at Drewry Bluff, and was then sent abroad for service on one of the Confederate cruisers running the blockade at Charleston, S. C. Young Mason went to Abbeville, a quiet town in France, where he applied himself assiduously to the study of his profession and in gaining a thorough knowledge of the French language, succeeding admirably in both.

About this time Capt. W. C. Whittle, a son of Commodore Whittle and nephew of Bishop Whittle, of Virginia, met Mason, who had passed his examination and secured his appointment as "passed midshipman." In October, 1864, he was assigned to a cruiser, gotten out from England for the Confederate Navy, and with Commander Waddell and other officers of the prospective cruiser, except Lieutenant Whittle, sailed from Liverpool on the consort steamer *Laurel* to meet their ship elsewhere. Captain Whittle writes:

"I was assigned to the ship as her first lieutenant and executive officer, and sailed from London on board of her under her merchant name, *Sea King*.

The two vessels, by preconcertion, met at the Madeira Islands, and, leaving there in company, sailed to Desertas Island, where the *Sea King* was christened and commissioned the Confederate States Cruiser *Shenandoah,* and the guns, ammunition, and equipment were transferred from the consort *Laurel* to the cruiser *Shenandoah,* which promptly started on her memorable cruise. Her officers were Lieutenant-Commander James I. Waddell, of North Carolina; W. C. Whittle, of Virginia, First Lieutenant and Executive Officer; Lieutenants, John Grimball, of South Carolina; S. S. Lee, Jr., Virginia; F. L. Chew, Missouri; Dabney M. Scales, Mississippi; Sailing Master, Irvine S. Bullock, of Georgia; Passed Midshipmen, Orris A. Brown, Virginia, and John T. Mason, Virginia; Surgeon, C. E. Lining, South Carolina; Assistant Surgeon, F. J. McNulty, District of Columbia; Paymaster, W. B. Smith, Louisiana; Chief Engineer, M. O'Brien Law, Louisiana; Assistant Engineers, Codd, Maryland; Hutchinson, Scotland; MacGreffery, Ireland; Master Mates, John Minor, Virginia; Coton, Maryland; Hunt, Virginia; Boatswain, Harwood, England; Gunner, Guy, England; Carpenter, O'Shea, Ireland; Sailmaker, Allcott, England.

"Under these officers and subordinates this gallant ship made one of the most wonderful cruises on record. She was a merchant ship which had not about her construction a single equipment as a vessel of war. Her equipment—such as guns, ammunition, breechings, carriages, etc.—were all in boxes on her decks, and these gallant officers and a few volunteer seamen from her crew and that of her consort were to transform and equip her on the high seas, and in all kinds of weather. None but the experienced can appreciate what a Herculean task that was. But it was enthusiastically undertaken and accomplished, and none were more conspicuous and untiring in his efforts to bring order out of chaos than young Mason.

"Our gallant little ship spread her broad canvas wings and sailed around the world, using her auxiliary steam power only in calm belts or in chase. We went around Cape of Good Hope, thence through the Indian Ocean to Melbourne, Australia, thence through the islands of Polynesia, passing the Caroline, Gilbert, and other groups, on northward through Kurile Islands into the Okhotsk Sea, until stopped by the ice. We came out of the Okhotsk and went up the coast of Kamchatka into Bering Sea, and through Bering Strait into the Arctic Ocean, until the ice again prevented us from going farther, so we turned, passed again through the Aleutian Islands, into the Pacific Ocean. By this time we had absolutely destroyed or broken up the Federal whaling fleets.

"While sweeping down the Pacific coast, looking for more prey, we chased and overhauled a vessel flying the British flag. On boarding her we found it was the British bark *Barracoula,* bound from San Francisco to Liverpool. This was August 2, 1865. From her captain we learned the war had been over since the previous April. The effect of this crushing intelligence on us can better be imagined than described. We found that much of our work of destruction to the whaling fleet of the United States had been done after the war closed, unwittingly of course, for from the nature of their work the whalers had been away from communication almost as long as we had, and were equally as ignorant of results. We promptly declared our mission of war over, disarmed our vessel, and shaped our course for England with well-nigh broken hearts. We journeyed around Cape Horn, and on November 6, 1865, arrived at Liverpool and surrendered to the British government through their guard ship *Donegal* by hauling down the last Confederate flag that ever floated in defiance to the United States, after having circumnavigated the globe, cruised in every ocean except the Antarctic, and made more captures than any other Confederate cruiser except the famous *Alabama.*

"After a full investigation of our conduct by the law officers of the Crown, it was decided that we had done nothing against the rules of war or the laws of nations or to justify us in being held as prisoners, so we were unconditionally released by the nation to which we had surrendered. But the authorities of the United States considered us pirates and in their heated hatred at that time would have treated us as such if we had fallen into their hands, so we had to find homes elsewhere than in our native land. Four of us (S. S. Lee, Orris A. Brown, John T. Mason, and myself) selected the Argentine Republic, in South America, and some time in December, 1865, sailed from Liverpool in a steamer for Buenos Ayres, via Bahia, Rio de Janeiro, and Montevideo. After prospecting a while, we went to Rosario, on Rio Parana, and near there bought a small place and began farming.

"As the animosity of the Federal government began to soften toward us, Brown and Mason returned home, Lee and myself coming some time later.

"On returning home Mason took a law course at the University of Virginia, graduated, and was brilliantly successful at his profession. He settled in Baltimore, and married Miss Helen Jackson, of New York, a daughter of the late Lieut. Alonzo C. Jackson, of the United States Navy. His wife, two sons and two daughters survive him."

When the *Century Magazine* was bringing out its series of war articles and "The Cruise of the *Shenandoah*" was wanted, Midshipman Mason was the only person who had the material for the sketch. It has been said that the story of these Confederate privateers reads like a romance of the sea. The record of Paul Jones is no more inspiring than the tale of Admiral Semmes and the *Alabama* and of Capt. James F. Waddell of the *Shenandoah.*

John Thompson Mason's "journal" appeared in print as "Leaves from the Private Journal of an Officer of the Confederate Steamer *Shenandoah*," in *Southern Society,* edited by Eugene Didier, of Baltimore.

Mason was always methodical, and although the youngest officer on the *Shenandoah,* was the only one who preserved his log-book, and kept a private journal during the entire cruise.

"BAYLOR'S BOYS."

Near Berlin, in the castle of Heros von Borcke, who served on the staff of both, the portrait of Stuart hangs above that of his Crown Prince. The owner answers criticism of this by asserting that Stuart, as a cavalry leader, had no peer in his generation.

In October, 1863, after the second cavalry fight at Brandy Station, while General Lee was moving his army around the right flank of Meade's army, with Stuart's cavalry protecting and concealing the line of march, the Twelfth Virginia, under Colonel Funston, had spent one morning in desultory skirmishing; and reaching the Warrenton road found Hill's Corps of infantry halted on a range of hills overlooking a bottom, on the farther side of which ran the Rappahannock River. The bridge and banks were held by a considerable force of the enemy, protected by rifle-pits enfilading the road for nearly a mile, and the hills beyond were fringed with cannon. It was a very unwholesome-looking road to ride on that day, so the whole army was halted till it could be cleared. The artillery was at work on both sides. The Twelfth Virginia were interested spectators for a minute, when a courier came dashing up with an order from General Stuart for the charging squadrons of Rosser's brigade to drive those people away. That honor belonged to Baylor's company from Jefferson County, with Company I from Warrenton supporting it, and there was quick mounting done and pushing for the front files, for an army were to be onlookers at their performance. Baylor's Light Horse and the Clark Cavalry disputed the claim to be the crack company of the Laurel Brigade. They were largely composed of wounded officers and men (and many boys) from the infantry service who re-enlisted as privates in these commands, and were nearly all splendidly mounted.

Out of the lazy grass, into the saddle, into the narrow and dirty road, by fours; drawn sabres, forward, trot, gallop—charge, and Company B was in a dead run across the valley for the rifle-pits, with cheers from our infantry battle line; first dropping shots, then volleys, then pandemonium in front as the river was reached—musketry smoke and the coming night obscuring all. On to the bridge and into fire, as well as smoke, for the other end was burned or torn away. Horses were pulled on their haunches, and from gallant Baylor and old Seth, at the edge, came the orders: "Halt! by fours, right about wheel, take the river!" And without a break in the ranks, or a moment's hesitation the little column turned, jumped their horses into the river and made for the other bank. Out of their entrenchment swarmed the Federals, not waiting for sabre stroke. Then came cheers from our infantry on the hills. In the midst of it all appeared Stuart, looking like a Centaur, his beard and his horse's mane in the air as he dashed to the bridge, Major Venable close behind him. The men took in the situation and one or two in the river held his bridle reins until the rest cleared up the blue coats on the other bank and formed company. Then Stuart was released, and riding up to Baylor he paid to him and his company a compliment as unique as it was substantial. Uncovering and bowing, he furloughed the whole command for thirteen days as a mark of his appreciation of their gallant conduct. Such a thing was probably never done before in the face of the enemy. The fact was that following the movement with his glass he thought the turn on the bridge meant a repulse and a disgraceful retreat of the flower of his command under the eyes of General Lee and a whole corps of infantry. Without a word he put spurs to his horse and dashed to the front to reform the squadron and lead the charge across the bridge. He had not even summoned his staff, and only Major Venable could reach him. One of the company now resident in Staunton relates this incident to illustrate the spirit and courtesy of the General commanding our cavalry, that matchless officer, J. E. B. Stuart, as well as the gallantry of his men and the mettle of the boys of Baylor's command.

"RICHMOND, VA., *October* 16, 1904.

"MY DEAR MRS. HULL:

"My sister handed me your letter and requested me to answer it. 'Boy Heroes'—I must confess I have never thought of being a hero during the war. I did what was told me. That is all that I can say. I am afraid if you start out to get every Southern soldier that was under eighteen years of age you will have a very large book. However, I will do what I can, and try and show what was my past. My first part in the war was as a Cadet of the Virginia Military Institute. In May, 1862, I left the Institute and went to Staunton, where we met General Jackson. After remaining there a day or two, we started with General Jackson's corps. Did no fighting. Were placed in line of battle at MacDonald, then went back into camp, and finally went to Franklin, in line of battle. Again no fighting. In July, 1863, I joined Colonel John S. Mosby's command, Forty-third Virginia Battalion of Cavalry, as a private; was made second sergeant of Company A; was promoted to second lieutenant of Company E; was never wounded or captured;

W. BEN PALMER.

OPPOSITE PAGE 168.

served until May 17, 1865, and was pardoned at Winchester on that date. I was sixteen years old while at the Virginia Military Institute, and when we took the trip with General Jackson and joined Colonel Mosby, was seventeen years old. I was mentioned in report by Colonel Mosby to General Stuart (see War Records); Colonel Mosby to Major H. B. McClellan, General Stuart's chief of staff, February 21, 1864: 'While all acted well, with but few exceptions, it is a source of great pride to bring before your notice the names of some whose conspicuous gallantry renders their mention but a duty and a pleasure. They are Captain and Lieutenant Chapman, Lieutenants Fox and Richards, Sergeant Palmer * * * .

"'(Signed.) JOHN S. MOSBY,
"'*Lieutenant-Colonel Commanding.*'
"Yours very truly,
"W. BEN PALMER."

IN CAMDEN STREET HOSPITAL, BALTIMORE.

I visited a great many wounded prisoners in the hospital in Baltimore, and found some of them beardless boys. It was dreadful to pass through rooms where these boys were lying side by side with men, many of whom looked as if they were unsuitable companions for school boys. Seeing what harm this arrangement might bring, I said to the doctor, "Do you think it is right to put those innocent boys with those dreadful men? You are a Christian and a gentleman, as well as a Union man. I cannot believe you are willing to kill the soul and think it your duty to save the body." He said, "You are right, madam, I will arrange it differently." I must give my testimony here to the perfect impartiality with which the two doctors I met, Dr. Waters and Dr. Dixon, treated the wounded. I thought I could even see a gentler expression toward the prisoners. While in the ward with Federals, the boys often whispered, "Divide with the Yanks," saying, "we are enemies in the field, but comrades in the hospital." They were always cheerful, uncomplaining and hopeful.

Of their courage and endurance one of the Seventy-eighth New York Volunteers (who enlisted in 1861, at fifteen*) said to me: "At the battle of Cross Roads we captured many boys of from fourteen to eighteen. Their feet were bleeding and sore from marching without shoes; they were cold, ragged, hungry, but they fought like heroes. They were so brave that they did not know when they were whipped." He added: "No man who was fighting in that war can say that the Southern soldiers were not courageous and honorable men. Those who stayed at home making money can scorn them."

Many of the Southern schools were closed, or if not the boys made the summer campaigns and in winter were always ready for emergencies. Even the professors went out, some as privates under their own student officers. Professor Gildersleeve, of the University of Virginia, now of Johns Hopkins, was wounded in battle, and often jestingly said his limp had more influence on his boys than his Latin. Four

---

***Frederick Flodt.**

brothers served gallantly and faithfully in the great Army of Northern Virginia from beginning to close of the war. Prof. Basil Gildersleeve was on staff duty in the field, and received desperate wounds in the battles around Richmond; the second, Benjamin, shared the well-won fame of the First Virginia Infantry; and the younger, Gilbert, was a captain of cavalry with Stuart. The father of these noble brothers was a distinguished Presbyterian divine, educator, and writer of South Carolina; and their grandsire was an officer in the Continental Army.

The boys of the North were not needed in the army. Many of them scarcely knew there was a war. The artillery was not thundering at their doors nor the incendiary torch threatening their homes. After the war one of Parker's Boy Battery was employed by a New York publishing house. An employee in the office, hearing a discussion on some battle, said, "There was quite a 'buzz' down there about that time, wasn't there?" The Southerner replied, "rather," and the conversation ended.

Northern colleges were not closed, as can be seen by a telegram from Mr. Lincoln to his son during the conflict, quoted from the *New York Herald* of September 18, 1892:

"ROBERT T. LINCOLN, Cambridge, Mass.

"Your letter makes us a little uneasy about your health. Telegraph us how you are. If you think it would help you, make us a visit.

"A. LINCOLN."

When we contrast the life of Northern boys resting at ease in the ordinary routine of life, with that of the young Southern soldiers called to defend that which they held most dear, at an age that needs all the safeguards of parents and home—cold, hungry, barefooted, worn with constant marches, sleeping in trenches or watchful sentry in the freezing nights; sick, wounded, prisoners; dying, the streams reddened with their blood; their bones whitening the battlefields where they fell—when we think of this we can hardly forgive the past. No result can palliate, no motive excuse it.

W. D. PEAK.

W. D. Peak, of Oliver Springs, Tenn., was born December 22, 1846, and volunteered in the Confederate service in August, 1861, as a member of Company A, Twenty-Sixth Tennessee Regiment. If there were any younger soldiers in the army as early as the time of his enlistment, Comrade Peak would like very much to hear from them. Give name, date of birth and date of enlistment.

ONE OF GEORGIA'S YOUNGEST SOLDIERS.

MATTHEW J. M'DONALD.

Matthew J. McDonald, nicknamed in his regiment "Mollie," enlisted in the summer of 1863 in Company I, First Georgia Cavalry, at the age of fourteen years. He served continuously with this regiment until January, 1865, when he was captured at Robertsville, S. C., and was kept a prisoner at Fort Delaware until about June, 1865. He went to Houston, Texas, in 1866, where he died of yellow fever October 1, 1867. The accompanying picture was taken in Texas a short while before he died, at the age of eighteen years. While in Texas he gave his life during the fearful epidemic of 1867 to the care of the sick. His life there during the epidemic was like his war record, full of brave deeds and self-sacrifice. "Mollie" McDonald, of the First Georgia Cavalry, was a brave, daring cavalier. [I regret I have no picture.—Ed.]

M. W. JEWETT.

Dr. M. W. Jewett, Commander of the Ivanhoe Camp, U. C. V., No. 1507, of Ivanhoe, Va., has a fine record as one of the youngest Confederate soldiers regularly enlisted. He entered the service of the Confederacy when he was thirteen years old, enlisting as a private in the Fifty-ninth Virginia Infantry, and served at Charleston, S. C., in Florida, and finally at Petersburg, Va. In addition to being commander of his camp, he is assistant surgeon on the staff of Gen. James Macgill, commanding the Second Brigade of the Virginia Division, U. C. V.

W. H. M'DOWELL.

W. H. McDowell was born in December, 1845. In August, 1863, he became a Cadet at the Virginia

Military Institute, and was killed in the charge of the corps of Cadets at the Battle of New Market, May 15, 1864. Only a few months at the Institute, Cadet McDowell had made a good standing, being twenty-fourth on general merit in a class numbering one hundred and eighty. As the corps charged through the fatal orchard, on Rood's Hill, he was shot dead, falling out of the line across a wounded comrade. A mere boy in age and in appearance, he offered up his life for his native land.

UNKNOWN.

Lieutenant Berkeley says: "As we entered Charlestown a small boy came out of a house and I called him to show me the way to the court-house. His eyes sparkled with excitement and he said: 'Take me up behind you, and I will show you.' When we got near the court-house he said: 'As soon as you turn that corner you can see it.' I said to the youngster: 'Now, you get off, for they will fire on us as soon as they see us and you might be killed.' He replied: 'Oh, please let me go along with you; I am not afraid.' I had to pull him off my horse, and as he struck the ground he called after me: 'I am going, anyhow.' And he did, sure enough."

UNKNOWN.

I spent July, August and September at Graeffensburg, a village between Gettysburg and Chambersburg. One morning a soldier rode up at full speed, leading the smallest, most beautiful pony I had ever seen. It was dappled grey, with a long white tail and mane, and paced as fast as the soldier's horse could gallop. I asked the soldier where it came from, and he said it had belonged to the son of some Rebel officer, who had come over with his father, and been either killed or captured. I tried to buy it, but it had to be corralled with other captured horses, and was not sold before I left. I hope Mrs. General Couch, who was staying in the same house with me, bought it as I advised. I often wonder what was the rider's fate. He must have been not over ten or eleven years old to be carried by such a small animal.

CAN'T LEAVE IF THE BATTLE IS TO BEGIN.

B. M. Zettler (of Eighth Georgia Regiment), Atlanta, Ga., writes of an incident that illustrates the spirit of our soldiers during the war for Southern independence:

"The seacoast and gulf cities had been stripped of every regiment that could possibly be spared, and the newspapers were appealing to all who were absent on furlough to return and save our beloved capital. Among such absentees was John Krenson, of Company B, Eighth Georgia Regiment, one of Bartow's 'beardless boys' from Savannah. He had been severely wounded in the memorable 'pine sapling' thicket at Manassas, and had never completely recovered from his wound. It was said, in fact, that his surgeon had pronounced him permanently disabled and unfit for further service in the field. But when the news came that McClellan's army was in sight of Richmond, he could stay no longer, and came to us, I think, about the time we took up our position at Price's farm, five miles from Richmond, and a short distance north of Nine-Mile road. The enemy's pickets were then less than three hundred yards in our front, and each succeeding morning they appeared in a new position and still nearer to us. As each day drew to its close, those of us on the picket line felt that the battle must certainly begin on the morrow. After a brief trial of his strength, Krenson had found that the surgeons were right. He could not stand active service, and a final discharge had been given to him. But he lingered in camp, and to each surprised inquiry as to why he did not go home he would reply with the question, 'Do you think the battle will begin soon?' and to the invariable answer, 'Yes,' he would add, 'Then I cannot leave now.' And so during two weeks he waited, thinking each day that the battle would occur ere the setting of another sun.

"Finally, on the 26th of June, upon our extreme left at Mechanicsville, the battle was on. Friday, the 27th, it raged furiously and McClellan's right wing was doubled back at right angles to his original main line, and what that cautious leader's next move would be not even the astute Lee was able to guess.

"Saturday came, and with it an order to General Magruder, holding our center across the Nine-Mile road, to make a demonstration against the enemy's lines in his front. 'Tige' Anderson's and Benning's Georgia Brigades were ordered forward. Companies A and B, of the Eighth Georgia, were ordered out as skirmishers to cover the front of the advancing column and drive in the enemy's pickets and sharp-shooters. Krenson was in his place in the skirmish line. The running fight was at short range, and almost at every step some one went down; and among the first to fall, a sacrifice to that attempt to 'feel the enemy,' was brave, proud John Krenson. An honorable discharge in his pocket, a sharp-shooter's bullet in his heart, that brave, young soldier boy was 'off duty forever.'"

AN OLD "GRAY COAT" OF "TAN COLOR."

During the reunion at Nashville there was on exhibition at general headquarters an old moth-eaten cloak made of some brown material and lined with red cloth that attracted more or less attention, and was left by the owner at the headquarters. A paper pinned to it stated that "This cloak was worn by Tom Triplett through the war. He was a member of Stewart's Black Horse Cavalry. Enlisted when only fifteen years old and was so small that he could not mount with his equipments or without assistance. Comrade Triplett was born and reared in Fairfax County, now Alexandria, Va., and now lives at Pine Bluff, Ark."

THREE BOY HEROES AT PERRYVILLE.

Three brave boys—neither one over eighteen—while struggling to plant their flag on the battery, were cut down. An eye-witness describes it as most wonderful. A hand-to-hand fight was going on; these boys plunged into the very jaws of death in the most heroic manner, grasping their flag-staff.

The last one was Sergeant Johnnie Carter, a son of Dan F. Carter, of Nashville, Tenn. When found he was firmly holding his flag, seeming loathe to give it up. Little did the brave boy dream that a death wound had seized him. He manifested a beautiful devotion to the Southern cause. Leaving a home of luxury, only son of doting parents, only brother of a loving sister, Johnnie laid his young life on the altar of his country. He died at Harrodsburg, Ky. His beloved surgeon, Dr. J. R. Buist, and his parents were with him, ministering tenderly.

T. G. BUSH.

T. G. Bush was born in Pickensville, Alabama. Entering the University of Alabama, he organized, in 1861, when he was thirteen years old, two military companies to aid the Confederacy. Two years later he was adjutant of the corps of Cadets who were odered into the Confederate service. In 1864 he became adjutant of the Fifty-second Alabama. In 1865 he entered the University of Mississippi and had among his instructors the late Justice L. Q. C. Lamar and Dr. L. C. Garland, late president of the Vanderbilt University. He graduated in two years, his older brother taking first honors and he second honors. Going into business, he organized the firm of T. G. Bush & Co., and in 1876 became president of the Mobile and Birmingham Railroad, which position he still holds. He was the first president of the Mobile Chamber of Commerce, and has also been the executive head of a number of important enterprises in the South.

CHARLES R. NORRIS.

Charles R. Norris, son of John Norris, of Leesburg, Loudoun County, Va., was born on the 12th of May, 1844, and killed at the First Battle of Manassas, July 21, 1861.

On the 11th of August, 1860, he entered the Virginia Military Institute as a Cadet from the county of Loudoun. In the spring of 1861 the war opened, and such a band of soldiers as the corps of Cadets, each one of them an accomplished officer, was of course at once called into service. The corps was ordered to Richmond; but young Norris, being one of the youngest in years and experience, was detailed, with some forty or fifty others, to remain as a guard to the Institute buildings and State Arsenal at Lexington. After a very brief period he and some eight or ten others were ordered to report to Gen. T. J. Jackson, then commanding the post at Harper's Ferry. He was promptly on the spot, and was assigned to duty as a drill-master to the volunteers then rushing, all untrained and undisciplined, at the call of their State. In the faithful and efficient discharge of the duties of his office he remained until the army, under Gen. J. E. Johnston, moved to the relief and support of General Beauregard, then about to engage the enemy in that first and terrible Battle of Manassas. Young Norris, though engaged as a drill-master, determined to go with the army. In the absence of the captain of one of the companies in Colonel John Echols's regiment, he was assigned to the command of the company. General Johnston's army reached the bloody battle-ground in time to engage in the thickest of the fight, and to contribute largely to that great victory. In this battle Cadet Charles R. Norris lost his life in command of his company, and in advance of his men, leading them in a charge with the rallying and encouraging cry, ringing out midst the smoke and din of battle, *"Come on, boys, quick, and we can whip them!"* Just uttered he was struck by a ball which took an oblique course across his breast, killing him, it is supposed, instantly, although his body was not found until the next morning, when, among the dead, mangled, wounded, and dying, it was discovered in a search over that ghastly field by an elder brother, who was also a soldier in that fight, but passed the battle-storm unharmed, and on many other fields struck manfully to avenge the death of that boy soldier and brother. Thus, belonging to no company, with his name not enrolled on any of the lists of the honored soldiers who fought and died for the "Lost Cause," did Charles R. Norris, only a little over seventeen years old, offer up his young life an oblation on the altar of his country.

JOHN BAILEY TYLER.

John Bailey Tyler, of Chicago, died in Chicago at the Alexian Brothers Hospital, after an illness of several weeks. Mr. Tyler, it is thought, was the youngest soldier in the Confederate Army who served throughout the war other than in the position of drummer boy. He enlisted when he was twelve years old as a cavalryman, serving throughout the war in D Troop of the First Maryland Confederate Cavalry. Mr. Tyler was born in Frederick, Md., in 1849. The fact that he was the youngest soldier in the command made him a pet among the officers and men. He was the son of Samuel Tyler, a lawyer of Frederick, and would have probably followed the same profession if he had not left his home to join the First Maryland at Winchester, Va., in 1862. During the war he was one of the most daring fighters, but among those who knew him most intimately it is thought that he was never injured. Since the war the veterans have heard but little of him, and they often wondered what had become of "the boy," as they called him.

ANOTHER "YOUNGEST SOLDIER."

E. G. Baxter, of Clark County, Ky., was born September 10, 1849; enlisted June 15, 1862; made second lieutenant July 5, 1863, Company A, Seventh Kentucky Cavalry, Morgan's command.

THAT'S WHY HIS CAPTOR OFFERED TO LEND HIM A BATHING SUIT.

An interesting story is told illustrative of the belief of Union soldiers that many women disguised themselves as men and fought in the Confederate Army. George W. Logan was only seventeen years old when he was taken prisoner in an attack on Fort Cannon. He was very slender, but deep-chested, and very girlish in his appearance, being fair, with high color and wearing his long, light-brown hair brushed straight back and unparted.

Taken to Point Lookout and later to City Point, he attracted the attention of an officer of the escort. The Federal officer treated the youthful prisoner with as much courtesy as circumstances permitted, frequently conversing with him. One day the officer asked to be told the truth regarding the belief among Federal soldiers that many women were serving in the Confederate Army, some of them being types of the best of Southern womanhood. Mr. Logan said it was not true, but he had heard, in common with others, that a few women had so served. The Federal officer was thoughtful for a while after the conversation referred to, and then urged the prisoner to forswear the Confederacy and go to the officer's Pennsylvania home. "I can arrange it without trouble," said the officer, "and my people will receive you and treat you like one of the family." A dozen times or more the Federal officer urged the point. "I subsequently learned," said Mr. Logan, "that he believed I was a girl, and that it was for that reason that he wanted me to go to Pennsylvania. He never intimated such a reason to me, but my information came in a way that seemed to be reliable, and then it was that I understood why, before our conversation about women, he had offered to procure me a bathing suit if I wished to go swimming at any time."

THE LATE EX-GOV. SEAY.

In the death of Ex-Gov. Thomas Seay, which occurred at his home in Greensboro, on Monday last, Alabama has lost an able and devoted son.

He had just reached his fiftieth year, and would, doubtless, have been crowned with further honors by the people of Alabama had he lived. Ex-Gov. Seay was but seventeen years of age when he enlisted in the Confederate Army, and served to the close of the war.

LEWIS HARMAN

Lewis Harman was born in Staunton, Virginia, December, 1845. He enlisted in the Fifty-second Virginia Regiment and was elected lieutenant. At the battle of Port Republic he was wounded, but when fit for duty joined the Twelfth Virginia Cavalry and was soon afterwards made adjutant; he was promoted to captain by General Rosser for gallantry. On the 5th of May he was wounded and captured in a fight between Rosser's brigade and Wilson's division. He was carried to Fort Delaware and was one of the six hundred Confederates who were selected by the Federals to be placed under the Confederate fire at Morris Island, South Carolina, in front of the attacking party. It was suggested by the United States officer in command that a flag of truce should be sent to the Confederates accompanied by one of the prisoners to explain the danger of his comrades. The prisoners unanimously declared that any one thus sent would urge the Confederates to fire regardless of their position, one very young officer saying, "Our lives are offered to our country and it matters very little by what shot we fall."* Captain Harman was, with his comrades, taken back to Fort Delaware, where he was held till the June following the surrender of Appomattox.

PELHAM

When the boy Pelham, with one gun, checked Burnside's advance on Fredericksburg, Stonewall Jackson exclaimed: "Give me more men and fewer orders; give me 50,000 *Pelhams* and I will subjugate the world!"

JAMES W. THOMSON

James W. Thomson was born at Berryville, Clarke County, Virginia, on the 28th of October, 1843. He entered the Virginia Military Institute in 1860, where his education was soon interrupted by the commencement of the late war. He promptly offered his services for the defense of his State, and was employed as drill-master until just prior to the Battle of Manassas, in which he acted as volunteer aide-de-camp to Gen. T. J. Jackson. For important service rendered in this action he received a flattering letter of recommendation from that General. In the fall of 1861 he was elected second lieutenant of Chew's Battery of Horse Artillery, and in February, 1864, succeeded to the command of the company. During the same year he was promoted, and commanded, with the rank of major, a battalion of horse artillery attached to Rosser's cavalry division until his death.

---

*His name was not given, but I guess.

Thomson was, by his early training and disposition, well fitted, even at the age of seventeen, when he entered the service, for the peril and hardships of a soldier's life. He was always devoted to out-door sports, and became, by constant practice, a perfect master of the horse. Tall and athletic, with a nature bold and daring, frank and generous in disposition—these qualifications, united to great physical strength and powers of endurance, presented a combination of soldierly traits possessed by few. As a commander of artillery he was remarkable for the prompt and daring manner of handling his guns. When his guns were not in action, it was frequently a habit with Thomson to join in the cavalry charge, and on such occasions attracted attention by his dash and almost reckless gallantry. It was while leading charges of this kind that he was wounded in the arm, on the 5th of April, 1865, and on the day following was killed. A gallant attack was made on this day by General Rosser upon a brigade of Federal infantry, which had succeeded in gaining the front of Lee's army, near Farmville, and during the fight a charge was made by Dearing's brigade. A desperate encounter ensued, resulting in the rout of the enemy, but at a great sacrifice of life; and General Dearing, Colonel Boston and Major Thomson all lost their lives.

Major Thomson acted in this fight with conspicuous gallantry, and fell where he was always found when duty called—at the head of the column. By his fall, his family and numerous friends sustained an irreparable loss, and his State was deprived of one of her most gallant sons.

COL. R. PRESTON CHEW.

PHILIP F. FRAZER

Philip Fouke Frazer was born in Lewisburg, Greenbrier County, Virginia, on the 22d of December, 1844, the youngest son of James A. and Sophia Frazer. In early childhood his gentleness of manner, his brightness and intelligence, rendered him a favorite with all who knew him. He was as modest and gentle as a girl, and yet possessed all those manly qualities which later in life, though still at an early age, made him the gallant officer and devoted patriot.

His early education was received at a girl's school in Lewisburg; here, when he reached the age at which boys were excluded from the school, so refined and gentle was he that his teacher said he should remain her scholar so long as he might choose to attend her school.

He was appointed a Cadet of the Virginia Military Institute in 1860, and reported for duty on the 19th of July of that year. He soon attracted the attention of his professors by his industry and brightness, and won the hearts of his comrades by his open, generous disposition and manly traits of character. In April, 1861, the corps of Cadets was ordered to Richmond, and proceeded thither under the command of General Jackson, to assist in drilling and disciplining the raw troops which were being concentrated there. Cadet Frazer remained at this camp of instruction for several months, as drill-master; but, though in consequence of his extreme youth and delicate appearance he could, doubtless, have readily secured a position which would have withdrawn him from the dangers of battle, the gallant young soldier would accept no such position, nor could he reconcile himself to the discharge of the monotonous duties of a drill-master when the soldiers of his State were confronting the enemy; and every day brought to him the intelligence of another battle fought. Leaving the camp of instruction then, he entered the Greenbrier Rifles, Company E, Twenty-seventh Virginia Infantry, as a private. In a very short time, though only sixteen years of age, he was elected first lieutenant of his company. So gallant was his bearing, and such the soldierly qualities which he had displayed, that when his regiment was reorganized he was elected captain of his company, which position he held for two years. In the spring of 1863 Captain Frazer was promoted major of his regiment. On several occasions, even while captain, he led his regiment into battle. In every battle in which his great commander, Stonewall Jackson, was engaged, except those around Richmond, when he was forced to be absent by sickness, he did his duty as a man and soldier. Through all he passed unscathed, until, at Second Manassas, he received a painful but not dangerous wound. In the battle near Wilderness Run, May 6, 1864, the very day on which he received his commission as lieutenant-colonel, this brave young officer fell, at the head of his regiment, shot through the head with a musket ball, and died while being removed from the field. Not an unworthy pupil of the noble Jackson, he laid down his life near the spot where that grand old hero received his death-wound. His name from childhood had been linked with all that is kind, loving, generous and true. At the time of his death he was but nineteen, perhaps the youngest officer of his rank in the whole army, yet the most distinguished officer of his regiment. Men of unquestionable courage and daring say that he was the most gallant and coolly brave man they ever knew. He lived without fear and without reproach, died as a true soldier, and is mourned as a devoted patriot, an efficient officer, a dutiful and affectionate son. The prop and support of his widowed mother and youngest sister, he unselfishly devoted to them the greater portion of the pay he received. In his last letter to his mother, received after he had gained his soldier's crown, he sent her all he had, hoping, with tender solicitude, that it might help her till he could send her more. His body was interred at Hollywood by the side of his idolized sister, Mrs. George E. Taylor. United in life, in death they were not divided—one monument telling their story.

GEORGE MURRAY GILL, JR.

George Murray Gill, Jr., of Baltimore, left Princeton College and entered the Confederate service in 1862. He joined the First Virginia Cavalry when they were about to charge a regiment of United States Regulars—when he had only a halter on his horse and was without pistol or sabre. He was wounded at Chantilly the day after the Second Battle of Bull Run. Was ill at Gettysburg and taken prisoner at Hagerstown. Spent five dreary months at Fort Delaware, and was then exchanged, and joined Mosby's command. He was wounded March 30, 1865, and died a few days later, in Virginia, after the surrender. His mother and sister started at once to nurse him, but as they crossed the Shenandoah River were told of his death. They made arrangements to take his remains to Baltimore, but after the assassination of President Lincoln the authorities stopped all trains and would not allow even a coffin taken through the lines. They sent up the mountain for the farmer, in whose house he had died, and gave him all they had brought from home for the wounded boy and learned from him the sad details of his death. He said: "George Murray Gill was glad to die for his country." His cousin, John Gill, read at his burial in Virginia the beautiful service of the Episcopal Church. His body was brought to Baltimore later and laid to rest in the family lot in Greenmount.

"On time's eternal camping-ground
 Their silent tents are spread,
And memory guards with solemn round
 The bivouac of the dead."

GRIM HUMOR

Ten days after the Battle of Gettysburg we were at Graeffensburg, formerly a water-cure, the bath-houses still standing, with a large pool of ice-cold water brought from the mountains by primitive wooden troughs. The walls were whitewashed and covered with inscriptions and names of soldiers of both armies. The following was most striking, showing the gaiety with which they went to the terrible conflict:

"July 3. General Lee's great circus will exhibit at Gettysburg tomorrow. General Early's famous equestrian troop will perform its usual feats of daring and agility."

[Signed by men of a Mississippi regiment.]

Under this:

"July 4th. In consequence of accidents to the performers, the troop has returned to Richmond."

[Signed by Northern soldiers, names and rank forgotten.]

This was enclosed in a circle and the owner of the place said it should never be obliterated.

THOMAS BOOKER TREDWAY

Thomas Booker Tredway, son of Judge William M. Tredway, of the Fourth Judicial Circuit, was born in Danville, Virginia, on the 13th of August, 1844.

In the month of April, 1861, being not quite seventeen years of age, he joined a volunteer company organized at Pittsylvania Court House, where he then resided. In May this company was ordered to Yorktown and attached to a Virginia infantry regiment under the command of Gen. John B. Magruder for about 12 months. Young Tredway was with his command in all service during this period, acting gallantly in the Battle of Bethel.

In the spring he was discharged from the army on account of his extreme youth and sent to the Virginia Military Institute, where he remained until 1863, when he rejoined his old company at suffolk and served through the summer campaign, and passing with it into Pennsylvania he was mortally wounded and left on the field of Gettysburg. It is supposed he soon died of his wounds, alone, as nothing was ever heard of him. He was not nineteen when he died—not old enough to have accomplished very much. Death prevented the fulfilment of a noble prospect of usefulness and distinction.

BASIL G. DABNEY

Basil Gordon Dabney was born on the 29th of October, 1847. He was the eldest son of Major William S. Dabney and Susan F. Dabney, *née* Gordon. He was born in Albemarle County, where his parents resided, and was taught at home under the instruction of a private tutor until 1859, when he was sent to the neighboring school of Captain Willoughby Tebbs, where he remained until Captain Tebbs entered the army, in the beginning of the war. After this he continued his studies at home until the latter part of 1864, when he entered the Virginia Military Institute, then located temporarily at Richmond. In February, 1865, thinking it his duty to go into service, he left the Institute and joined Thompson's Battery of Horse Artillery, which was then disbanded for the winter. About the last of March he received orders to report at Petersburg. He reached Richmond on the 2d of April,—the day before the city was evacuated,—and finding his company not yet reorganized, together with his captain, James Thompson, and other members of his company, he joined temporarily the Second Virginia Cavalry, and was with that regiment on the retreat.

On Thursday, the 6th of April, 1865, when a number of Confederate baggage-wagons were attacked near Farmville, in Prince Edward County, the 2d Virginia Cavalry was ordered to their defense. A severe fight ensued, and in it young Dabney received a wound in the right leg, just below the knee. The surgeon to whose care he was entrusted deemed amputation necessary. Owing to the carelessness of the surgeon (who was intoxicated) the chloroform was improperly administered, and the poor boy never rallied from the operation, but died that evening,—April 6, 1865,—aged seventeen years and nearly six months.

Basil Dabney when at school had proved himself a hard student. He was naturally fond of reading and study, and was always at the head of his classes. By his teacher he was deemed a youth of very great promise. His family and friends had looked with hope to the fulfilment of this promise. But it was not to be so. Only four days a soldier, his life was borne away on the dying groan of the Southern Confederacy.

JOHN OPIE

John Opie, only seventeen years of age, a son of Hiram Opie, of Staunton, Virginia, was given a gold medal on the field of Manassas by Jefferson Davis for distinguished bravery. After fighting furiously all day he pursued the retreating columns, capturing a fine horse which he presented to his major. He fought gallantly until the end of the war and has written a most interesting and amusing account of his experiences, "A Confederate Cavalryman."

BOY FROM BEE'S BRIGADE

Opie says: "When Bee's brigade was driven from the field a boy was shot in the forehead and died without a groan. He did not tell us his name but simply asked if he could fall in with our company. Poor boy, he died like a hero, among strangers."

EX-CONFEDERATES IN CONGRESS

Among the ex-Confederates in Congress who took action on the death of General Gordon were John W. Maddox, of Georgia, who enlisted in the Confederate Army at the age of fifteen, and served as private until the end of the war; and Robert W. Davis, of Florida, who entered the Confederate Army at the age of fourteen, and surrendered with the army of General Joseph E. Johnston, at the close of the war.

JOHN GILL

General John Gill, of Baltimore, entered the Confederate service at eighteen. His experience during the war has been graphically told by himself in his "Reminiscences of Four Years as a Private Soldier." General Fitzhugh Lee writes of him as follows:

"John Gill, of Baltimore, served at my headquarters and near my side for the greater part of the war from 1861 to 1865. He was one of a number of heroic Marylanders who left their homes to join and do service on behalf of the South. I had him detailed to report to me because I had been informed that he was a good soldier and performed all the duties confided to him in a satisfactory manner. I first assigned him to duty as a courier and afterwards promoted him to be sergeant in the Division Signal Corps. I found him active, vigilant, energetic, and courageous in the various encounters between my command and the Federal cavalry. I am correctly quoted as having stated years ago that I would be glad to lead in a fight 5,000 men like John Gill against 10,000 of the enemy. He should know what he is writing about [referring to General Gill's book], because whenever the opportunity occurred his place in the war picture was near the flashing of the guns."

PETER R. BEASLEY

Peter R. Beasley, son of Dr. Jas. A. Beasley, was born near Huntsville, Alabama, on the 16th of July, 1844. In his boyhood he was noted for his firmness, self-reliance, and energy; which traits characterized him in a marked degree as he approached manhood.

He entered the Virginia Military Institute in the fall of 1860, and remained there until the suspension of the school in the spring of 1861, when he went with the battalion of cadets to Richmond, and served there as a drill-master until the First Battle of Manassas.

Returning then to Huntsville, he joined the Thirty-fifth Alabama Infantry, in which regiment he served as a private for some time, and was then promoted first lieutenant. In this capacity he served until, at the Battle of Corinth, in 1862, he received a severe wound in the leg, which obliged him to return to his home for some time. Returning from his furlough, he served with his regiment in all its duties, an efficient and trusty officer, until the 4th of July, 1864. On that day he was engaged in throwing up breastworks near Marietta, Georgia. During the progress of the work Lieutenant Beasley mounted the parapet to see that it was more efficiently done. Repeatedly warned of his imminent danger, he continued cool in the discharge of what he considered his duty, until he was shot down by a ball breaking his leg.

Persistently refusing to have the limb amputated, he would not consent to have chloroform administered by the surgeons who examined his wound unless they gave their word of honor that they would not amputate the limb while he was unconscious. He was removed to Forsyth, Georgia, where after lingering for three weeks in intense suffering, borne with soldierly fortitude, he died on the 25th of July, 1864, aged twenty years and nine days.

Lieutenant Beasley's decided character, clear and vigorous intellect, and purity of morals gave promise that he would have become a man of mark had he escaped the perils of war, *sed dis aliter visum est.*

Deeply beloved by family and friends, the following tribute to his memory, from the pen of a lady friend, must show, as best it can, that estimation:

"The memory of our noble patriot boy
Shall build the temple of our country's fame,
Each one a classic stone, a sacred name.
And here, in after-years to come,
We'll bring our little ones to learn
The names that make us great."

ALEXANDER LYLE

The subject of this brief sketch was born October 14, 1844, at the place called Timber Ridge, in Charlotte County, Virginia, then the residence of his maternal grandfather, Dr. A. D. Alexander. It was in this part of the State, not far from the graves of Henry and Randolph, that young Lyle passed his early years and received his early schooling. From the first he manifested a fondness for books, having learned to read when only three years old. Alexander was the son of A. A. and Mary Q. Lyle, both of Scotch-Irish blood, and descended from ancestors who formed a part of the colony that settled the Valley of Virginia.

In the year 1861, Lyle, then a lad of hardly more than sixteen, entered the Military Institute at Lexington, where he remained under the manly tutelage and strict discipline of that well-known institution until the cadets were ordered to the front, and, abandoning their tents and barracks and the daily spectacle of mimic war, followed their brave leader to the scene of actual conflict. Fired with the same patriotic thirst for distinction, Lyle was eager to be of the number of those ardent young spirits who were taken to the field; but, in consequence of his immature years, he was denied this privilege (as he regarded it), and advised to bide his time, and in the meanwhile to be content to serve his country in other and less conspicuous ways. He joined the command of Colonel Mosby. This was before he had reached his seventeenth birthday. He continued dutifully at his post till the summer of 1863, when he was mortally wounded in a cavalry fight at Warrenton Junction. In this condition he fell into the hands of the enemy, by whom he was carried to Alexandria, where he died in hospital in the month of June of that year, and was decently buried in the neighboring cemetery. Just one year had elapsed since his devoted brother, Captain Matthew Lyle, fell in battle at Gaines's Mills, after greatly exposing his person, and while leading his company in a gallant and successful movement against the enemy's works.

The younger Lyle died composedly in his bed about two o'clock in the afternoon, surrounded by ministrations of kindness and sympathy. Conscious, and notified by the United States chaplain, who attended him to the last, that the change was approaching, he asked that he might not be left alone. When it came, he met it with fortitude and resignation, and passed away without visible pain or struggle. The evening before he had had a long and free conversation with a minister of the gospel, in which he spoke more fully than he had up to that time ventured to do on religious subjects. The truth of the gospel and his own deep need of it seemed apparent to him. He expressed a determination to continue to pray for mercy and salvation, as he had done. He dwelt with fondness on the remembrance of his father, his friends, his home, but uttered no complaint that it was his lot to die among strangers. He was tenderly cared for to the sad end, and received the last offices of Christian benevolence at the hands of those with whom resentment had melted into admiring pity. Alexander Lyle sleeps side by side with his Northern adversaries, and, when flesh and heart were failing, received this unsolicited and unlooked-for tribute from the stranger, "A brave and noble young man."

REV. H. C. ALEXANDER, D. D.

BERKELEY MINOR

Berkeley Minor was born October 6, 1842, at Edgewood, Hanover County, Virginia, the son of Lucius Horatio and Catharine Frances Berkeley Minor. After education in private schools, mostly at home, he entered the University of Virginia in October, 1859, winning honorable success during two sessions, and in July, 1861, enlisted in the Rockbridge Artillery. Of this celebrated company he continued a member until April 15, 1864, when he was made a sergeant in Company I, First Regiment Engineer Troops (Col. T. M. R. Talcott), Army of Northern Virginia. The following November he was made lieutenant in the Second Regiment and assigned to Company H, which he commanded until the close of the war, the other officers being absent sick, or on detached service. He surrendered at Appomattox, thus closing a career as a soldier honorable throughout for gallantry and patient fidelity to duty, and one to which his friends never recur without pride.

Mr. Minor remained on his plantation in Hanover for some years after the war, but in 1871 became a master in the Episcopal High School of Virginia, near Alexandria, which position he retained for eight years. While there, in 1875, he married Susan Watson Fontaine, daughter of James Fontaine, of

Hanover. Since 1879 Mr. Minor has held a professorship in the Virginia Female Institute at Staunton, the position he now occupies.

L. M. B.

G. JULIAN PRATT

G. Julian Pratt entered the military service of Virginia, a youth of eighteen, as a private in the Sons of Liberty, a company composed of students of the University of Virginia, commanded by Captain James Tosh, of Petersburg. This company formed a part of Major Carr's battalion under General Harper, and saw their first service in the capture of Harper's Ferry. After a short campaign the students were ordered to their Alma Mater and disbanded. In July, 1861, he enlisted in the service of the Confederate States, as second sergeant of the University Volunteers, commanded by Capt. James Parran Crane, now Judge Crane, of St. Mary's County, Maryland. They reported to General Wise and were assigned to the Fifty-ninth Virginia Infantry as Company G. The men and officers of this company were honorably discharged July 13, 1862, but he, reporting to General Wise at Norfolk, Virginia, was by him commissioned captain and assigned to enlisting and organizing a company of marine artillery for the defense of Roanoke Island. He was captured February 9, 1862, and confined on the prison ship *S. R. Spaulding* until paroled. After his exchange, with the consent and by the advice of General Wise, he reported to Colonel John D. Imboden and enlisted in the First Regiment of Partizan Rangers. In connection with Francis Marion

Imboden he raised, inside the enemy's lines, a company of cavalry, armed and equipped from the Federals, and which became Company H of the Eighteenth Virginia Cavalry, and December 11, 1862, Julian Pratt was commissioned first lieutenant and F. M. Imboden, captain. At this time the Partizan Rangers were transferred to regular service, and Colonel John D. Imboden promoted to be brigadier-general. Lieutenant Pratt served gallantly until the close of the war, was wounded twice and had five horses shot under him—three in one battle, that of Winchester. He commanded the company in 1863, and in 1864 was made captain of Company A, Eighteenth Virginia Cavalry. He commanded the squadron composed of A and H companies of Imboden's brigade, Lomax's division of cavalry, in the Army of Northern Virginia.

FRANCIS MARION IMBODEN

Francis Marion Imboden was a cadet at the Virginia Military Institute, April 16, 1861, and was then eighteen years of age. He was assigned as drill-master, and served in this capacity at Camp Lee, Richmond, Virginia, until some time in the early fall of 1861, when he was ordered to General Henry A. Wise, commanding in West Virginia, who assigned him to the command of a company known as the "Ben McCullock Rangers," which was one of the components of the Fifty-ninth Virginia Volunteers. He continued in command of the company until the Battle of Roanoke Island, when he was transferred to the First Virginia Partizan Rangers, and in connection with Lieutenant G. Julian Pratt, he enlisted a company of cavalry inside the lines of the enemy, and was commissioned captain, December 11, 1862. An educated soldier and extremely gallant man, he commanded this company frequently on detached service, attacking the enemy's outposts, and made a splendid reputation for himself and his command until captured in the Battle of Piedmont, June 5, 1864. He remained in prison at Johnson's Island until the close of the war.

P. H. GRANDY

P. H. Grandy, son of A. W. Grandy, Esq., of Norfolk, Virginia, entered the Virginia Military Institute in October, 1859, being sixteen years old. Went into service as drill-master with the Corps of Cadets in April, 1861. Was appointed first lieutenant in a North Carolina regiment, and served as such until killed in the battles around Richmond, in June, 1862, in the nineteenth year of his age.

JULIAN B. HARDY

Julian B. Hardy, son of P. A. Hardy, Esq., of New Orleans, Louisiana, was born in that city on the 18th of March, 1842. In August, 1858, he entered the Virginia Military Institute, together with his younger brother, H. F. Hardy, and made such excellent progress in his studies that at the end of his first session he stood third distinguished in his class. During the next session the brothers were called home, and at the opening of hostilities Julian enlisted in the Crescent Regiment, commanded by Colonel Marshall J. Smith, and served with it faithfully performing his duty as a soldier. For conspicuous bravery at Shiloh he was promoted to a lieutenancy, which position he held until killed at Murfreesboro, Tennessee, January 20, 1862, in the twentieth year of his age.

RANDOLPH BRADLEY

The subject of this sketch was born in Page County, Virginia, on the 28th of May, 1842, and was connected on both sides with the best families in the State. When young Bradley was three years of age, his father, William Bradley, Esq., removed to the West, and settled in the interior of Missouri. Here Randolph attended district schools, showing considerable proficiency in mathematics. Among his schoolmates he was remarkable for his love of truth and high sense of honor. In his nineteenth year he entered the Virginia Military Institute, this being in the autumn of 1860. The following April he was sent with the Cadets to Richmond to act as drill-master. In this service he was engaged for three months. He then determined to enter the service of his adopted State, which had seceded about this time; but, upon reaching Memphis, Tennessee (whither he had gone with dispatches for General Floyd), he found it impossible to get through the enemy's line, and therefore returned to Smyth County, in southwestern Virginia. Volunteering here in the Smyth Blues, he was with them in all their marches and other military services until the latter part of December, 1861, when he received an appointment as second lieutenant in the Confederate States Army, and was assigned to duty in the Fourteenth Louisiana Infantry. In the course of a few months, Lieutenant Bradley was promoted first lieutenant and adjutant. At the battle of Williamsburg he acted as aide-de-camp to General Pryor, was slightly wounded, and so distinguished himself for his coolness and gallantry that he was mentioned in the general's report of the battle as deserving promotion. At the Battle of Seven Pines he was promoted captain in the Fourteenth Louisiana, then commanded by Col. R. W. Jones. In this capacity he served until he fell mortally wounded, leading his company in battle, during the great Seven Days' fight around Richmond, on the 27th of June, 1862.

The regiment was ordered to storm a battery, and in so doing was cut to pieces, every officer save three, and two-thirds of the privates, being killed. Colonel Jones, in speaking of Captain Bradley, says, "He displayed great courage and coolness on the field of battle, and lost his life by no rash act of bravery." He was taken from the field of carnage to the house of Colonel Fry, in Richmond, where he was tenderly cared for by loving friends, the Rev. Dr. Minnegerode offering him spiritual comfort in his last moments. He expired on the next day, June 28, 1862, and his remains now sleep in Hollywood Cemetery, with the proud city he died to defend his only monument.

His immediate family were no laggards in patriotism—one brother losing his life in the Mexican war, another dying a lieutenant-colonel in the Confederate Army, and a younger brother being a soldier in the Missouri State Guard.

Laying down his life before he had reached the age of manhood, Captain Bradley had yet endeared himself to friends, and proved himself so worthy, that they shall ever dwell on his noble deeds and glory in his memory. In personal appearance he was tall and commanding; his finely formed head was covered with dark-brown hair, and his deep-blue eye was penetrating and intelligent. Strong in frame, bold in disposition, he was kind, benevolent, and humane; and in his sense of right and regard for duty was as unyielding as the fiat of Heaven.

HENRY GOODRIDGE SPEED

"Henry Goodridge Speed, youngest son of John Joseph and Anna Strachan Speed, was born at Roseland, Granville County, North Carolina, August 19, 1845. He received his primary education at the 'Belmont Select School,' and in 1862 entered as a cadet the Virginia Military Institute. The writer of this notice, then on his way to the Institute, met Speed for the first time at Lynchburg, and traveled with him, and many others who were hastening to become 'Rats,' to Lexington. Speed was the life and soul of the party, ready and anxious for any adventure which promised fun and amusement, and provided there was a little danger so much the better. When we arrived at Lexington, as a matter of course we became legitimate prey for the old cadets; many of whom imagining that a residence of twelve months at the Virginia Military Institute supplied all deficiencies of mother wit, would, upon the announcement of the arrival of a new cadet, immediately proceed to his quarters to amuse themselves with his greenness. Many of those who came to Speed on this occasion for wool went away shorn. So brilliant were his repartees, and so confounded his would-be tormentors at having the tables turned upon them in this unexpected and unprecedented manner, that we, his more timid comrades, escaped with comparatively slight punishment. He became at once a universal favorite, and when, at the end of a year, he severed his connection with the Institute, there was not a man in the battalion who was not distressed at his going. After leaving Lexington, he joined the Third Virginia Cavalry, and in the spring of 1864 was transferred to the First North Carolina Cavalry. On the 21st of August, 1864, in an engagement at Poplar Springs Church, near the Petersburg and Weldon Railroad, he received a shrapnel-shot in his heart, and his spirit took its flight for the happy mansions prepared by a kind and merciful Father for those who die in defense of the Right and of Truth.

"One of his last acts is illustrative of his character. His application for leave of absence had been approved, and he was preparing to visit his friends and relations at home, when a comrade received information that his wife was at death's door, urging him to come at once if he would see her alive. Speed, with his usual generosity, immediately gave his furlough to his comrade, and it was whilst serving in this comrade's stead that he met his death; thus crowning a life of honor and nobility with an act of which an angel might be proud.

"He was recommended for promotion, but was killed before he could receive the fruits of his gallant conduct on many a hard-fought battlefield.

"Three bosom friends left the Virginia Military Institute together, gallant, noble, chivalrous. Charlie Haigh died leading his regiment to victory at the Battle of the Wilderness; his peer, Gardner McCance, manfully serving his piece, sank to rise no more; and Henry Speed, while serving for a friend received a bullet through his heart."

ERASMUS STRIBLING TROUT

Erasmus Stribling Trout, of Staunton, Virginia, was the eldest child of Hon. N. K. Trout and Matilda Stribling, his wife. He was born in April, 1844, and was only seventeen when the Civil War occurred. With the earnestness of his nature he became interested in the Confederate cause and would at once have entered the army, but his friends feared that his delicate constitution could not withstand the hardships and exposures of field service. He was sent to the Virginia Military Institute in 1861, with the view of completing his studies and with the hope that the admirable physical training there enforced would render him somewhat robust. He remained there until the corps was disbanded, in July, 1861. Without delay he attached himself to the Fifty-second Virginia Infantry in the capacity of a drill-master, wherein he displayed great efficiency.

He returned to the Virginia Military Institute in January, 1862, when the Institute was opened by order of the Governor of Virginia. He was a member of the Corps of Cadets when the latter was ordered to march with General T. J. Jackson's army to Franklin.

When he left the Virginia Military Institute he entered the ranks of the Fifty-second Virginia Regiment. Colonel James H. Skinner, then commanding, appointed him the sergeant-major of the regiment. "For conspicuous gallantry in the battle of Cedar Mountain," August, 1862, he was promoted to the rank of second lieutenant in Company H, Fifty-second Virginia Regiment.

After the battle of Sharpsburg he was further promoted to the rank of first lieutenant. During General T. J. Jackson's brilliant Valley campaign, in 1864 (in which the Fifty-second Virginia Regiment acted a most conspicuous part), he was commissioned captain of Company H.

He was present and participated with his regiment in all the battles fought by Pegram's brigade, from Cedar Mountain till the close of the war, with one exception, when sickness compelled him to be absent.

He was in command of the Fifty-second Virginia Regiment at the surrender of the Army of Northern Virginia at Appomattox Court House, and signed the parole for the men of his regiment. What more honorable record could be made of a soldier than that his name is enrolled with that patriotic band who followed their noble chieftain, General Robert E. Lee.

BOYS OF CANE HILL COLLEGE

In a sketch of the services of Captain Pleasant Buchanan in the Confederate War, I. Mont Wilson, of Springfield, Missouri, gives the following:

"Pleasant H. Buchanan was Professor of Mathematics of Cane Hill College, Arkansas, when the war began. When the first call for troops was made by the State, a company of boys from the college and the surrounding country was at once organized, and Pleasant Buchanan was elected captain, the President of the College serving as a private. * * *

"During the second day's fight, Captain Buchanan, his first lieutenant, Paton Inks, and some of his men penetrated the Federal lines, were captured, and sent to prison on Johnson's Island. In the summer, when Captain Buchanan and Lieutenant Inks were exchanged, they found themselves without a command, so they made their way to northwest Arkansas and attached themselves to General T. C. Hindman's army. * * *

"Captain Buchanan fought as a private in Captain Garl's (Cane Hill) company of the Thirty-fourth Arkansas Infantry at Prairie Grove and was slightly wounded in the side, the ball passing through his canteen. The following spring he received a commission from the War Department to raise a cavalry company of Partizan Rangers. * * *

"The squads and scouts left in northwest Arkansas not coming South as expected, Gen. W. L. Cabell detailed Captain Buchanan to take eleven picked men and horses and go to northern Arkansas and bring out the men. His instructions were to avoid all towns, Federal posts or large bodies of Federals, gather up all squads or individuals, not to do anything to alarm the Federal posts, and to avoid any engagement till across the Arkansas River. This was a hazardous undertaking, as at that season of the year the Arkansas River was only fordable at a few places, and every dugout, canoe, or boat of any kind had been burned by the Federals, except at large towns, where guards were watching the river. There was a chain of posts along the north side of the river from Little Rock to Van Buren, and on the south side from Little Rock to Fort Smith. Every mill and village had a post and scouts passing daily. The worst feature was that the leaves being off the trees, there was no forage at all, and neither meat nor bread for the women and children. It took a level-headed, cool man, with plenty of nerve, to carry out these instructions, and that was the reason General Cabell selected Captain Buchanan for the important undertaking. We had no trouble until we came near Waldron, forty miles south of the Arkansas River, with a post of a thousand men. We had been riding quietly on the road only two or three hours when we came on Federal scouts in a house near the road. They hustled around lively with their guns, and we expected to have hot work in a few seconds; but Captain Buchanan rode straight up to the house and inquired if it was the military road to Fort Smith, and by his coolness made them believe we were Federal scouts going to Fort Smith. He rode quietly back to us and moved down the road in an ordinary walk till we were out of sight and hearing, when we rode rapidly toward Fort Smith for an hour. Traveling all that night by the north star, we struck the river nearly opposite the mouth of Big Mulberry. We hid our horses in a deep slough that made into the river, fed and rested them, while some of us slept and others reconnoitered the river for a crossing.

"We decided to try it on a bar just above the mouth of Big Mulberry. Just as the sun went down we rode into the river, and made it without getting into swimming water; thence four miles north to the road from Ozark to Van Buren, through underbrush, brambles, brier thickets, and a very dark night. It did not take long to tear down the telegraph wire and drag it out in the woods in sections. We then took all the roads leading in the direction of Cane Hill, traveling hard to cross the Fayetteville and Van Buren road before daylight, so we could get to Boston Mountain and rest during the day and reach Cane Hill the next night. We crossed over the mountain and reached Fola Gray's, the first house we dared to approach after crossing the river. We learned that Major Wright was in command of a post at Cane Hill, composed of Federal 'Pisi Indians' and negroes. We circled around this place, and all separated, going two and two together to our respective homes, and then began at once to get word to all the scattering men and squads in Benton, Washington, and Madison counties to be ready to start south on a certain date, our rendezvous to be the Twin Mountains, in Benton County. I went with Captain Buchanan to his home. His brothers, William and James, were at home on sick leave. They wanted to go south with us, but had no horses, and there were none to be bought in the country, the Federals having taken all.

"We had learned that Major Wright's headquarters were at Mr. James Hagood's, and that his horses and some of the other officers' horses were kept in stables about one hundred feet from this house, with a guard near by. The captain decided that we could go down there the night before we started, get their horses, and mount his brothers. So we four went and let the fence down around the lot, but ran on to a guard in the lot; then we had to get away quietly. My sister was at White McClellan's, only a quarter of a mile away, so I went by to tell her good-by, and the captain went with me, as Charlie McClellan was going with us. While there Misses Emma Hagood and Amanda Hinds told me that they had tied Major Wright's horse to the fence just in the rear of the dwelling, where we could get it. I asked the captain if he would allow me to go and get it, and I did, and we all four returned to his mother's and left before daylight, moving out in the barren timber toward Rhea's Mill, and stopped to feed our horses before starting for the Twin Mountains.

"William Rhinehart and Guy Blake, two of the escort, had joined us, and in thirty minutes more we would have been on our way and they would not have been able to come up with us. Our horses all had their bridles off. The captain was lying down on some leaves with a paper over his face. William Buchanan had procured a plug of a horse and James had gotten a mule.

"When I first saw the Federals they were about one hundred yards away, deployed in line. I called to the boys, and each one sprang to his horse. As we did this they began firing and charged us. My horse and the captain's mare stood with their heads near together. As I sprang into my saddle and wheeled my horse, the captain was standing in his stirrup, with his right leg nearly in the saddle. Rhinehart and I ran together, and we had gone about one hundred yards when the captain's mare dashed by us. I was satisfied then that he was shot. Will and Jim Buchanan were shot before mounting. They ran at Jim to shoot him while he was trying to bridle his mule, and he fought one of them with his bridle for fifty yards before he could shoot him.

"I have heard that I was censured as being the cause of their death by taking that horse. It is possible we could have gotten away without their making such an effort to find us if I had not taken the horse. It was the suggestion of the captain that we get the officers' horses to mount his brothers, William and Jim Buchanan, and we were only prevented by the guard. I did not offer to go for the major's horse till the captain cheerfully gave his consent. I also heard at that time that the negroes had reported to the Federals that we were there and put them on our trail. Major Wright's orders to the troop of Federals sent after us were to take no prisoners, as I have learned since.

"I was in Captain Buchanan's class in college, was in his infantry company till captured, again was one of the first to join this cavalry company, was in his mess from that day till he was killed, and I never saw a more perfect Christian gentleman. With my intimate and varied association with him I never heard him utter a word that could not have been spoken in the presence of a lady. He was as brave as the bravest, very cool, and never got rattled in a fight. He was a model officer and soldier, and was respected by all of his men. I never saw but one soldier refuse to do anything he told him. In his cool, quiet way he convinced that fellow that he had better do it, and do it quick. He was so modest and unassuming, it was only those who were intimate with him that knew his real worth and merit."

The brutality of the Federals after these men were killed is beyond precedent. In a letter from Mrs. ——— to Comrade Wilson, author of the foregoing, she states:

"In regard to the death of the Buchanan brothers I will tell you what I remember of the circumstances. It is painful to me, even at this day, to recall that scene. Mrs. Buchanan requested some of us to go and care for the bodies and keep the hogs from getting to them. Mrs. ———, of Little Rock, and I volunteered to go for her sake. We had gone about half way to our old home place—about a mile—when we heard the scouts coming in with the bodies, and we waited for them to come up. The bodies were stripped of all clothing save the undergarments. We asked the captain to take them down to their mother. He would not consent, but said he wanted us to go down with them to Boonsboro. We got into the ambulance with the dead boys lying in the back part, so powder-burned and blood-stained that we could not recognize them. They drove at full speed all the way, yelling and shouting: 'Hurrah for Captain Buchanan!'

"After arriving at Boonsboro ——— and I went to a residence until they had washed the faces of the dead boys, then we recognized each one. They were shot in the face and head, but no other violence that I remember, except that Captain Buchanan was stabbed in the side three or four times. The Federals then took them back up home to their mother. Two of the old citizens went with us in a separate hack.

"They were dressed in their graduating suits, which Mrs. Braden got from their hiding places in the attic. As far as I know, everything was conducted in order at the burial. I did not go. * * * Never can I forget that moonlight ride with those dear boys thrown in like butchered swine, and the yells of those negroes and Indians!"

The other lady who accompanied them on that sad mission recalls the awful event, and writes of it minutely, even quoting the words of participants. She mentions, for instance, that while an Indian, Redbird, was looking at Jimmie he said: "That was one brave man. I hate to kill him; but I have to, as he kill me."

I regret having to give this incident, but I think it might emphasize the objection many thoughtful persons have to the use of semi-civilized savages, *en masse,* in warfare. In this case Major Wright commanded Pisi Indians and negroes, hence the terrible outrage.

Dr. Paul J. Carrington told me that in one of the battles in the West, where the South was victorious, the Indians became so intoxicated by the carnage, that they rushed over the battlefield, scalping both dead and wounded, friend and foe. After this the Confederate Government only employed her Indian soldiers in companies or regiments, to guard the frontier. Even when fighting singly, however, they still show marked characteristics. Just before the Battle of Gettysburg, General Howe's cavalry passed

Emmitsburg, where I was staying, and some stragglers falling out, hid in Doctor Sharb's barn. The next day General Stuart's cavalry unearthed the sleepers and there was quite a skirmish in the lane in front of the house, the bullets pattering on the roofs of the porches where we were standing. The Stuart men were victorious and the enemy led a rapid chase down the lane. A young Indian from New Mexico was one of the pursuers, riding a mule, with long black hair flying. Uttering piercing war-whoops, he tore madly along the road, brandishing a long pike and leading three horses he had captured. "The ruling passion strong in death," he looked exactly like one of Cooper's "red men."

EDMOND PENDLETON MAJOR

Edmond Pendleton Major, of Culpeper, Virginia, one of four brothers, all of whom, except the killed and maimed, were at the post of duty at the time of the surrender, was only eighteen years of age when he joined the University Volunteers under Captain Crane. That he was all aglow with the spirit against which neither students nor professors were proof is shown by a letter to his father—after his enlistment. "The Washington College boys are in the field; the Emory and Henry; the Hampden-Sidney students passed through last Saturday, a fine company and well equipped, but ours will be the finest company ever sent out, composed of the flower of Virginia and all the South." He also wrote, showing he felt the deep responsibility: "Duty calls and I must go. My comrades are going, why should

I remain while they are fighting for our liberties. If I have done wrong you and mother must forgive me, because I think it my duty to go. If I survive I will have the gratification of knowing I had been one of my country's defenders. If I am to fall, I can say 'Thy will, O Lord, be done.'" After asking for other articles of his soldier's outfit he added: "Tell mother to send me a small Bible or Testament, which is the most important of all." In July the Volunteers were sent to West Virginia, a hard service even for Confederate soldiers, and for many days at a time they had neither tent nor shelter nor food, except green corn growing in the fields, of which Edmond said he had eaten ten ears at one time. Finally the company of sixty-five muskets, reduced to eleven men through sickness and battle, was disbanded and Edmond returned home, only to fall ill with typhoid fever. Before he was entirely recovered he joined as an independent volunteer the Twenty-sixth Alabama Infantry and marched to Yorktown, where Colonel O'Neale wrote, "He had shown great courage and coolness." He was subsequently made adjutant of the Twenty-sixth Alabama, and was distinguished for gallantry at the Battle of Seven Pines. His death was singular and touching. The fighting was over except now and then a random shot. He was lying under a tree talking to Colonel O'Neale and Lieutenant Halsey when a rifle shell passed between them, stunning Colonel O'Neale, wounding Lieutenant Halsey, and killing Edmond instantly without even breaking the skin. "He was brave and cool in battle, moral and correct in his deportment, faithful and true in the discharge of his duty," said one who saw him fight and saw him die.

THE SECOND MARYLAND AT COLD HARBOR

The following extract from the account of the Battle of Cold Harbor, by Major R. L. Poor, on General Breckinridge's staff, was given me by a member of the Independent Maryland Regiment who lost his foot just before the attack on Culp's Hill. He begs me not to mention his name, as he "did so little," but it is very difficult not to do so. He says that when the attack occurred the soldiers of the Independent Maryland were lying down in a depression of ground anticipating no attack, as they were in reserve, and the surprise was so great many men were shot in their blankets.

"To ——— ———, Esq.

"Baltimore.

"DEAR SIR: Enclosed please find herewith the sketch of assault at Cold Harbor, June 3, 1864, and the very prominent, gallant, and successful part taken by the Independent Maryland Regiment of Infantry, and credit due them for the repulse of the victorious assaulting columns of the enemy after Hancock's divisions of Birney and Barlow had overrun and captured our line of entrenchments and the men of Breckinridge's division occupying them. They were marching unimpeded to our rear and the position occupied by the Independent Maryland and General Breckinridge's headquarters for the night.

"At 4 a. m., June 3, 1864, the picked divisions of Hancock's corps, 5,000 strong, ran over our entrenchments and captured them and 300 of our men, also McIntosh's battalion of artillery supporting them. They then continued their charge to our rear until they encountered the Independent Maryland, 300 men, which was the only force we had to protect our rear and check the victorious charging columns. We were awakened out of a peaceful and sound slumber at 4 a. m. by a sharp and startling cry from some one in the Maryland Regiment: "My God, look at the Yankees! They are almost on top of us!' and truly they were, for in the dim, hazy light of coming dawn we could discover the compact mass of blue-coated men yelling and charging upon us. In shorter time than I can relate it the Independent Maryland was to a man on its feet, loading and firing into the very faces and breasts of the surging foe, at point-blank range. This fire was so galling and fatal that the charging columns seemed to melt away before it. Soon their dead and dying were strewn thickly over the field; their columns faltered, were crushed and in full retreat to the rear in an endeavor to seek safety within their own lines. But they were assailed on the right by Cook's North Carolina and on the left by General Finnegan's Florida brigades and fearfully punished. The men of the Independent Maryland Regiment were thus made heroes and covered with imperishable fame and glory and saved our lines. The loss was so great to the enemy that the ground between us looked like a lately cleared woodland covered with stumps.

"General Grant stated his loss to be 10,000 men and that the results did not justify the slaughter, as they were all in favor of General Lee and demonstrated that he could not dislodge General Lee's army from behind their earthworks by direct assault. General Grant, however, ordered another general assault the evening of the same day, but his men, with one accord, refused to move out of their lines and thus rebuked their commander-in-chief for the morning's reckless slaughter. We plainly saw their lines forming about 5 p. m. for an advance, and after leaping over the breastworks stop suddenly and remain in line for some time, and then go to the rear and disappear. This movement we could not understand and consequently it was much commented on.

"A few years after the war General Hancock was en route to Fortress Monroe by our steamer line. I was seated in my office at Union Dock when one of his aides came in and asked me if I were Major Poor and at Cold Harbor when the assault was made; and when I replied 'Yes,' he asked if I would go on the steamer and see General Hancock, as he wished some information in regard to it. General Hancock received me cordially and asked what forces and troops we had in reserve when his command overrun and captured our works. I replied: 'None, unless we might call the Independent Maryland Regiment of 300 men, which was a few yards in rear of the main line of entrenchments, a reserve.' He replied: 'Your statement is to me almost incredible, and I could not believe if you had not so stated it, because Generals Barlow and Birney reported that after carrying your works they advanced some distance without resistance and suddenly encountered a large reserve force, which gallantly attacked them with great vigor, and inflicted severe loss upon them and speedily forced them to relinquish the ground and works they had captured and seek shelter within their own lines.' He said further: 'I had instructed Generals Barlow and Birney, if they succeeded in breaking through the enemy's lines, to hold them at all hazards and I would support them with my entire force and the whole army if necessary. It is therefore hard for me to believe that such gallant and experienced officers and leaders of troops should have been so terribly deceived and commit such an unfortunate blunder.' Hence we can appreciate now, from General Hancock's statement, what an important part the glorious 300 of the Independent Maryland Regiment took in the defense of the Cold Harbor lines and the repulse of the assaulting columns.

"I regret to have spun so long a yarn. 'An old Confederate' never knows where to stop his war talk. Craving your pardon and trusting I have not wearied you, I am,

"Yours truly,

"R. L. POOR,

"Late Major, Engineer of Breckinridge's Staff.

"Major Poor is mistaken in regard to Finnegan's brigade. It was to our right and rear several hundred yards. I remember distinctly looking back as we made the charge and seeing them marching in good line to our assistance. I think he is mistaken in regard to the artillery being McIntosh's battalion. I was told by Colonel Stribling it was Rice's battery of his battalion.

"D. RIDGELY HOWARD."

AN UNKNOWN CONFEDERATE SOLDIER BOY

[The courage of the Confederate boys is almost equalled by the modesty of the "Veterans." They are willing to give their "lives" for country only.

Writing to veterans known to have acted their part nobly, they reply: "*I* did nothing. Put——in." The following is a letter from men of that ilk, well and favorably known in Confederate records.—ED.]

"October 26, 1904.

"MY DEAR SWEET COUSIN: Oh, no—a thousand times no! There is nothing I would not do at your behest except that. Such a thing about myself is impossible. No Confederate soldier should applaud himself for anything he did, since his only proper feeling should be gratitude to God that he had the opportunity and privilege of discharging a plain and simple, but glorious, duty. Yet I am glad that you have found pleasure in the work you have undertaken. I can say truly, the only war history I have read with pleasure is Henderson's "Life of Stonewall Jackson," and this only because it is the work of an unbiased hand in which such plain and even justice is meted out to both sides as must necessarily enhance the respect and esteem of the adversaries each for the other, and thereby promote their self-respect. There is another book by Major Robert Stiles, called 'Four Years under Marse Robert,' which I read with pleasure, it being his own reminiscences of what he saw and helped to do, and it is told modestly and naturally. I am sure you will not misunderstand me, but lest you might I will say again I am glad that you have essayed to write the book, and it will give me pleasure to read it, as I am not in it, for that would give me positive pain. I not only can not recall one single thing I did to evoke the mildest praise of the most generous, but I always feel my cheek mantle with shame that I should have gone through four whole years of active, daily service in the field, and never received a single scratch. Surely a man with that opportunity, who did not lose several legs and arms and have at least one eye shot out, might now be said *never* to have been 'in it.' Again I beg that you excuse me.

"Your affectionate cousin,

"J. T. B."

HENRY D. BEALL

Bushrod C. Washington, of Charlestown, West Virginia, writes of his comrade:

"The following incident, which is well vouched for, will give some insight into the resourcefulness, self-confidence, and audacious courage which rendered the services of Henry Beall so valuable to 'Jeb' Stuart and Gen. R. E. Lee.

"General Lee, desiring to know something of the numbers and movements of Pope's army before making the attack known as the Second Battle of Manassas, Henry Beall was directed by General Stuart to scout in the rear and on the flank of his antagonist. He went, accompanied by Sergt. Jas. H. Conklyn, of Company B, Twelfth Virginia Cavalry. After numerous adventures within the Federal lines, they arrived after dark at the residence of a gentleman, known to Beall, close by a Federal encampment, part of Pope's army. It was from this family that Beall expected to obtain valuable information. When they got close to the house they heard the music of a violin, and could see through the window that there were Federal soldiers inside dancing a cotillion with the young ladies. Sergeant

Conklyn, supposing that the game was up, asked Beall what they should do. 'We shall go inside and dance a set with them,' Beall replied without hesitation; 'and if you don't feel like going, you can stay by our horses until I return.' But Conklyn preferring to stay by his companion, in whose resourcefulness he had implicit confidence, they hitched horses, and together approached the house by the front door, and, without drawing arms, quietly entered the room among the dancers. The surprise of the parties within can better be imagined than described. 'You were having such a good time,' Beall remarked to the Federals, 'that we thought, if there is no objection, we would come in and dance a set with you.' Conklyn says he himself kept a close eye on the Federals' muskets, which were stacked in a corner of the room, while a set was made up, in which Beall danced with one of the ladies of the family whom he knew. It goes without saying that during that set he obtained the information he was seeking. The cool audacity of the adventure had exactly the effect upon the Federals that Beall had counted upon. They, of course, supposed that the house was surrounded by Confederate cavalry and that resistance was useless. 'It was a solemn dance,' says Sergeant Conklyn, 'on the part of the Yankees, who expected to be marched off as prisoners of war.' Beall and Conklyn quietly withdrew from the room and rode off without molestation."

WHO "SUE MUNDAY" REALLY WAS

"I have been very much interested in Captain Ridley's letters and especially his account of the Southern heroines. I have waited for some one to correct an error he made in regard to 'Sue Munday.' Captain Ridley certainly knows enough about Gen. John H. Morgan's command not to have left the impression that 'Sue Munday' was a heroine only in name. As I understood it, 'Sue Munday' was Jerome Clark, son of Hon. Beverly L. Clark, of Franklin, Kentucky, who died while United States Minister to Guatemala, C. A. Jerome Clark was a member of Company A, the old squadron, and was noted for his remarkably fine and feminine features. The boys in camp frequently called him 'Sissie.' They dressed him up one day as a lady and introduced him to General Morgan as 'Miss Sue Munday,' thinking that they could fool their dashing chief, but that was never done. After enjoying the joke with the boys for a while, he said to them: 'We will have use for Miss Sue'—and he did, too."

T. D. CLAIBORNE

T. D. Claiborne, son of Colonel L. Claiborne, was born in 1847. Entered the Virginia Military Institute in January, 1854. Resigned. Entered military service in April, 1861, as captain of Eighteenth Virginia Infantry. Promoted major, in 1863, of an independent battalion of infantry; lieutenant-colonel in 1863. Mortally wounded, and died in 1864, aged seventeen.

RANDOLPH CARY FAIRFAX

Randolph Cary Fairfax was the son of Dr. Orlando Fairfax and great-grandson of Dr. Bryan

Fairfax, who inherited the title of Lord Fairfax. His mother was the daughter of Jefferson Cary and Virginia Randolph. He was born in Alexandria and from his infancy was remarkable for an almost womanly beauty. His eyes were hazel, his hair of a golden brown, his features regular and his complexion brilliant. These soft beauties made him a most attractive child and as he grew older he developed a manly form which, though not tall, was of noble and graceful bearing. From his earliest years it was said of him, "Randolph is actuated by a desire to do his duty." In the fall of 1857 he entered the Episcopal High School of Virginia and in June carried off the honors in every class with medals and certificates of proficiency. In 1859 he took the highest honor at the High School, the "gold medal," besides many smaller prizes. On the 12th of August, 1861, he enlisted as a private in the Rockbridge Battery, then commanded by Capt. William N. Pendleton. For our knowledge of his career as a soldier we are indebted chiefly to the familiar letters from his messmates and himself, which contain a continuous description of Jackson's wonderful campaigns as they appeared to a boy of eighteen years of age in the ranks. He fell at his gun on the 13th of December, 1862, at the Battle of Fredericksburg.

HENRY JENNER JONES

Perhaps no battle of the war was comparatively so widely spoken of as the one fought at New Market, in the Valley of Virginia, in May, 1864. Though a complete victory, Breckinridge, with a force slightly exceeding three thousand men, utterly routing Sigel with more than double that number, it would have sunk into insignificance, happening as it did just at the time of great and important battles of the Wilderness and Spottsylvania Court House, but that a romantic interest was attached to it from the gallant participation of the "boys" of the Virginia Military Institute; and a thrill of sorrow sent through the Southern land, re-echoed even from our foes, at the death of the eight brave boy-soldiers, too young to have known the horrors of war. The subject of this sketch was one of this band.

Cadet Henry Jenner Jones, son of Thomas S. and Mary E. Jones, was born in King William County, Virginia, on the 10th of March, 1847. When sixteen years of age, in August, 1863, he was entered at the Virginia Military Institute, becoming a member of the fourth class. With this class he pursued his studies, passing successfully the intermediate examination, until the 11th of May, 1864. On that day the corps was ordered to join Breckinridge's army at Staunton.

Jenner, for so he was called, was, like many of his comrades, too young to perform efficient service, but like them moved by love of home and country, roused by a contagious enthusiasm, and, more than all, stung to his heart's core by the death of his elder brother, who had been killed at Seven Pines, he went with his comrades to battle for his State, to avenge his brother's death. In the disposition of his forces on the field of New Market, on Sunday morning, May 15, General Breckinridge threw the Corps of Cadets into his second, or reserve line, designing, if possible, to keep them from the dangers of the engagement, but the exigencies of battle and the determined enthusiasm of the gallant corps prevented the carrying out of this design. The regiment immediately in their front breaking under the galling fire, they closed in and filled up the gap, giving material assistance in turning the tide of battle. But before this glorious moment, before they had come into direct contact with the foe, death had thinned their ranks; a shell passing over the first line burst just at the junction of the flanks of C and D companies, killing the orderly sergeant of D company and three privates. Jenner Jones was of this number. His face lit up with the fire of battle, he fell ere his hand had been raised to avenge his own and his country's wrongs.

Of his character, a brother says: "It was just forming, and gave promise of much future usefulness. He was of a warm, affectionate disposition, securing thereby the love of all who knew him well. He eminently displayed those Christian virtues of integrity, truthfulness, honor, and courage, for which his Welsh ancestry were noted; and yet it bemourns me to state he never made an open confession of his faith in Christ. This, indeed, is the saddest point in his life; yet we do hope that the eminently pious influences of his sainted father had early impressed his mind for good, so that even without our knowledge he had secretly consecrated himself to the service of his Master."

THE YOUNGEST ON RECORD

Comrade G. K. Crump, of Tunica, Miss., writes: "I have seen several claims made as to the youngest Confederate veteran, but I met recently one who, at time of enlistment and amount of actual service rendered, surpasses any record I have yet seen. George S. Lamkin was born at Winona, Miss., November 3, 1850. He joined Stanford's Mississippi Battery, at Grenada, Miss., on August 2, 1861, and at Shiloh, before he was twelve years old, was badly wounded. At Chickamauga he was wounded twice, once quite seriously. Mr. Lamkin was very tall for his age when he entered the service, and is now a man six feet and four inches tall. He lives at 880 Adams Street, Memphis, Tenn. Mr. Lamkin is of a retiring disposition, and was averse to my mentioning this matter, but I think it should be known as a matter of history.

CONFEDERATE HEROES

Col. A. K. McClure, in his address on the subject of erecting a monument to Gen. Robert E. Lee at Gettysburg, considers that Cushing and Armistead indicated more clearly the high-water mark of American heroism than did any one else. I think while this is a statement which is very pleasing to Virginians, it is not literally true, for they were only two among many. I think the following letter addressed to Lieutenant Carter Berkeley will show that Virginia could boast many other heroes who had clearly attained this high mark. Lieutenant

Berkeley is a second cousin of Gen. Robert E. Lee, and was a brave officer in the Confederate service.

Captain Parks, writing to Lieutenant Berkeley, October 14, 1901, says:

"In *The Confederate Veteran* I noticed your inquiry concerning the death of Col. I. B. Thompson, of the First Arkansas Regiment (Infantry), killed at Shiloh. I presume you mean Lieut.-Col. John Baker Thompson, of Little Rock, Ark., formerly of Virginia, who was some two years president of St. John's College.

"I dined with Colonel Thompson some time about the last of March or first of April, 1862, at the Gayoso Hotel, at Memphis, Tenn. At that time I was eighteen years of age and he twenty-four, and I was senior first lieutenant of heavy artillery, Hoadley's Arkansas Battery, and shortly thereafter succeeded him as captain of said battery. After dinner, as I was to take passage on a Mississippi steamer, Colonel Thompson walked with me to the boat. On the way to the boat he was making many inquiries touching my captain's proficiency in military tactics. I remember he asked me this question: 'Where is the position of the lieutenant-colonel and major in time of action?' (He was then a lieutenant-colonel and the impression was a great battle would soon be fought at or near Shiloh, his command being a part of the Confederate forces to be engaged in the expected battle.) Laughingly I said: 'Why, Colonel, ask me something not so easy.' He said: 'You do not know, sir; nor does your captain!' 'Supposing I did know,' I answered, 'as shown by diagram in Hardie's "Tactics?"' 'Ah,' said he, 'just as I expected. Your answer is incorrect, but I do not censure you, because the answer to that question is not in General Hardie's "Tactics." He failed to translate that from the French tactics, of which I have a copy.' He then explained to me what the French tactics set forth—their places are in time of action on the right or left in line of battle 6 and 12 (or 15) paces, and explained the reasons therefor. Knowing him to be a brave and chivalrous Christian gentleman and scholar, I looked him straight in the eyes, thinking it could be only a few days until he should be in the impending conflict, and said as we were shaking hands to part: 'You surely will not thus unnecessarily expose yourself in the coming engagement, will you, Colonel?' He answered: 'I will most certainly do my whole duty, sir!' With a voice of sadness I said: 'Then, my dear Colonel, I will never see you again. You will be killed in that battle. May God bless you! Farewell!'

"The battle came. It proved to be one of the bloodiest and most important and withal, perhaps, the only battle fought out as planned, in the whole Civil War. Great indeed was the loss we sustained there. Perhaps the greatest loss was that of Albert Sidney Johnston, who was considered by President Jefferson Davis as one of the greatest generals in America. There, as I had predicted, Colonel Thompson fell upon the right and at the head of his regiment. He lived four days, though pierced with four (some reported eight) balls in his breast."

Borne to the rear by his men, as he passed through the ranks he encouraged others, telling them how sweet it was to die for one's country. The enemy remained in possession of the field, so that Colonel Thompson died within their lines. His grave was marked by his orderly, who had accompanied him, and after the war his remains were brought to his native State of Virginia and deposited in Hollywood Cemetery at Richmond.

In the cyclorama of the Battle of Shiloh the death of Colonel Thompson is marked as one of the principal events. He was called the Havelock, or Christian soldier, and was the idol of his command.

COL. JOHN BAKER THOMPSON AND HIS BOYS

The First Arkansas Regiment consisted, in part, of the students of St. John's College, Little Rock, from fourteen to nineteen years of age. Its president was Col. John Baker Thompson and its professors were afterwards officers in the regiment. Colonel Thompson opposed secession, not as a question of right, but of expediency, and used every effort to influence his boys against it. Captain Fellows, one of the professors, afterwards an officer of the First Arkansas, subsequently district attorney for the city of New York, spoke against secession and Colonel Thompson gave the boys a half-holiday to hear it, and said it was the most eloquent speech he had ever heard, and "most convincing." Nevertheless, when Virginia seceded he sent in his resignation and offered his services to his State. When reproached with his apparent inconsistency he said, "I was opposed to secession; but when it comes to a fight, every man must 'shinny on his own side.'"

The parents and friends of the students persuaded him to remain in Arkansas, saying they would in that case consent to their boys enlisting, as they knew he would consider the boys committed to his charge a sacred trust. Shortly after the enlistment the First Arkansas was ordered to Virginia and joined General Holmes's brigade, which was ordered to Manassas to support the right wing. The march was made in such unprecedented time that the regiment was complimented on the field by President Davis and General Beauregard, and orders were given that they might call themselves "Jackson's Foot Cavalry," and inscribe that on their banner. It is said this is the origin of the name given Jackson's soldiers.

The men were not allowed to halt on the march; the roads were dusty and the weather warm, and they suffered terribly from thirst. When the battlefield was reached the command was thrown into the forefront of the fighting. Almost directly in front of the regiment was a spring of cool water, completely covered, however, by the guns of a Federal battery. This tempting spring, so near and yet so far, was exceedingly tantalizing to the thirsty men, and finally, when human nature could stand it no longer, three young boys, each under sixteen, whose names, unfortunately, have been lost in the flight of time, volunteered to get some water from the spring. With a lot of canteens strung over their shoulders the three young heroes started on their perilous journey. As soon as they came within range of the Federal battery it opened on them, and a perfect hail of canister and grape swept the field. The three lads reached the spring uninjured and quickly filled the canteens, while their comrades watched with breathless interest, expecting every moment to see them struck down. Suddenly, as if by magic, the fire from the battery ceased. Then as the boys started on their return to the regiment an officer on horseback rode out from between the guns of the battery, and, lifting his hat, waved it to the boys, while a hearty cheer broke from the throats of the cannoneers. The officer had discerned the mission of the lads and given the order to stop firing. The cheer was responded to by the thirsty Confederates, and a few minutes later they were pouring the refreshing water down their dusty throats.

Possibly at Kennesaw, when the men and boys of the First Arkansas Regiment saw the unfortunate wounded boys in blue in danger of a horrible death in the burning woods, they remembered the incident of the first great battle of the war.

NOTE.—"Many of our readers know of the battle of Kennesaw Mountain, Georgia, which was fought on June 27, 1864. On that fateful day General Sherman made a front attack up General Johnston's lines, and was repulsed with awful slaughter, leaving many thousands of his dead and wounded on the ground, the entrenched Confederates suffering comparatively little loss.

" 'It was during this battle,' says General French, 'that one of the noblest deeds of humanity was performed that the world has ever witnessed;' and we are sure that no one will be found to dispute the statement. We follow the narrative: 'Col. W. H. Martin, of the First Arkansas Regiment of Cleburne's Division, seeing the woods in front of him on fire and burning the wounded Federals, tied a handkerchief to a ramrod, and, amid the danger of battle, mounted the parapet and shouted to the enemy: "Come and remove your wounded; they are burning to death; we won't fire a gun till you get them away. Be quick!" And with his own men he leaped over the works and helped in the humane work. When this work was ended a noble Federal major was so impressed by such magnanimity that he pulled from his belt a brace of fine pistols and presented them to Colonel Martin with the remark: "Accept them with my appreciation of the nobility of this deed. It deserves to be perpetuated to the deathless honor of every one of you concerned in it; and should you fight a thousand other battles, and win a thousand other victories, you will never win another so noble as this." '

"Is there anything in history that better illustrates the higher meaning of chivalry? It is fit to be matched with the conduct of young Kirkland, of South Carolina, who, at the risk of his own life, loaded himself with canteens full of water and climbed over the fortifications at Fredericksburg while the battle was raging, that he might relieve the thirst of his wounded foes. It is even finer than the magnanimity of Sir Philip Sidney at Zutphen, or than that of the French cuirassier at Waterloo. If the people of the South should ever forget it they would be guilty of a piece of unpardonable baseness.

"We have often wished that some one with competent literary skill would gather up into a bright and attractive volume the more notable instances in the war between the States, in which the better side of human nature found its expression. Such a volume would do more to abate the lingering prejudices between the North and the South than all the efforts of all our statesmen. Some things should be cast into oblivion; but whatever furnishes a lesson in forbearance, in high-mindedness, in Christian courtesy, is an inalienable part of our inheritance, and should be passed on to our children."

LETTER FROM COLONEL THOMPSON AFTER THE BATTLE OF MANASSAS

"CAMP MCGREGOR, *August* 15.

"MY DEAR SISTER:

"Were it not for the pressing duties and worrying inconveniences of this life, I would write you often. We were under arms all yesterday expecting an attack. Let it come! I was at the fight at Manassas. Our brigade gave the *coup-de-grace*. We converted their retreat into a rout, after marching in quick (presto, presto) time, seven miles, to reinforce the left wing. We marched a mile under their rifle battery but without damage. Our rifled cannon made their field officers take the fences at the very first discharge. Lindsay Walker, who manned the Pawnee, fired the first shot from our brigade, and it fell right into a close column retreating in fair order, scattering them in every direction. I have seen nothing of H. C.—would I might have an opportunity to do him some favor. * * *

"J. B. T."

FIRST ARKANSAS BOYS

I have but few names of boys of St. John's College, Arkansas. I give those I have been able to obtain—Beall, Ray, and Carl Hempstead. Carl Hempstead, scarcely seventeen at the breaking out of the Civil

War, but with a military training, volunteered to fight in the ranks, at the Battle of Shiloh, and fell far in the van, at the close of the second day's engagement. He was a typical Southern boy, with all the enthusiasm of youth and the courage of the born soldier, and is one of the heroes who sleep on the sacred ground of Southern battlefields.

"Rose" Thibault was killed instantly at Pilot Knob, Mo., September 27, 1864, receiving a Minie-ball in the chin, and was found with his face to the foe, only a few steps from the fort, where he fell in front of the charging forces. A brave and noble boy, only eighteen at the time of his death, having enlisted at fifteen.

Of John J. Baggett it is said that "he was thought to be the finest-looking soldier in Texas." William Osborne, with eighteen of his battery, was captured at Island No. 10, and died in prison at the North. Of the others I know nothing but the names—Peyton D. English, F. Pratt Oates, Thos. W. Newton, Capt. Wm. Fulton Wright, Ivan Pike, George E. Dodge, Frank T. Vaughan, John T. Boyle, John Wesley Moore, Mack Hammett, Matt Hudson, David Dodd.

LETTER FROM CAPTAIN JOHN R. FELLOWS

"MILITARY PRISON, JOHNSON'S ISLAND,

"*November* 4, 1863.

"MRS. S. R. HULL, Baltimore, Md.:

"MY DEAR MADAM—Your letter of 29th ult. to Brigadier-General Beall having made me acquainted with your name and residence furnishes me an opportunity which I have long desired, of acquainting the relatives of Lieut.-Col. J. B. Thompson with some particulars of his death. He was, as you are probably aware, major of the First Arkansas Regiment from its organization, and served in such capacity through the first year of the war. In the latter part of February, 1862, the regiment was ordered from Virginia to Corinth, Miss., where it reorganized and your brother was elected to the position of lieutenant-colonel. At the Battle of Shiloh the regiment was one of the first in action, and about ten o'clock Sunday morning it made three successive charges upon a strongly fortified position. It was in the second of these and while leading the command (being some distance in advance of the line) that Colonel Thompson fell.

"His conspicuous position and gallant bearing evidently drew upon him the fire of sharp-shooters, as he was struck almost simultaneously by seven balls. He was immediately carried to a hospital in the rear and placed under the charge of skilful and attentive surgeons. The duties of my position in the regiment prevented me from seeing him (after he was wounded) that day, and at night we bivouacked some three miles away. The next day I visited him in company with Colonel Fagan. He bore his painful wounds with more of heroic fortitude and uncomplaining patience than I have ever witnessed in any other person, conversing cheerfully about his own condition and giving full and minute directions as to the disposition to be made of his effects. The management of these he entrusted entirely to Colonel Fagan, and the family in Virginia have been fully informed of what his instructions were and how they were executed.

"We were compelled to leave him in the hospital on our retreat, as he could not bear removal. One of our own surgeons remained with him, and both from him and from the Federal surgeons he received every care and attention. He died on Thursday morning, April 10, and was buried near the hospital, his grave being marked. He died as he had often expressed a wish to do, upon the field of battle, meeting his fate with the fortitude of a true soldier and the calmness of a Christian.

"Colonel Thompson was my intimate and cherished friend—nay, more, my ideal and model. I never knew a man of such fine and irreproachable character, and he carried the graces of his Christian calling into every act and operation of his life. The vices that always prevail in camp did not even assail him and had no influence upon him except to stimulate his efforts for their removal. He moved constantly in an atmosphere of integrity, purity and virtuous action—an atmosphere of his own creation. His influence for good over the men of the regiment was something wonderful—the loud oath, coarse jest, or obscene story was never repeated in his presence. He was the idol of his command, and the roughest and most hardened soldier became subdued and gentle in his presence and eager to accomplish his wishes. He ruled, too, almost alone by the power of his noble example, being firm but never harsh. His men *loved* him too well to disobey him.

"One of Colonel Thompson's remarkable characteristics was his unvarying cheerfulness. Always genial in manner, sportive yet brilliant and instructive in conversation, he was the delight of the circle which in camp or bivouac used to gather around

JOHN BAKER THOMPSON.

OPPOSITE PAGE 240.

him and listen to the music of that social life—melody that we, alas, shall hear no more.

"Many of us lost dear friends in the bloody struggle of those two days, and by the side of the streams and under the trees in the dark forests of Shiloh are lying now, in their last sleep, those in whom our hearts were bound up. But when it was told us that Colonel Thompson was dead, all private griefs seemed forgotten in a contemplation of the great loss *all* had sustained. As for myself, I felt that it was irreparable. I used to sit in his presence as a child before a loved teacher. Possessed of the charm and fascination that cultivated intellect always imparts, enjoying with a keen zest the society of others and always adding to its interest by his own accomplishments, where shall we find another so worthy our love? To the regiment he was at once an officer, a friend, and an oracle.

"It is with feelings of sad and mournful satisfaction that I offer to his memory this brief, imperfect tribute, evoked by the thoughts of him which crowd upon me tonight.

"I shall be very glad to hear from you, and if I have omitted to state anything respecting his military career and death it will gratify me to state it.

"Believe me very respectfully your friend,

"JNO. R. FELLOWS,
"Staff Brig.-Gen. Beall."

COL. JOHN BAKER THOMPSON

Col. John Baker Thompson was born April 6, 1836, at Vacation, in Amherst County, Va., the son of Judge Lucas Powell Thompson and his wife,

Susan Caroline Tapscott. He was of distinguished Colonial ancestry. Through his father he was the grandson many times removed of Hon. Benjamin Harrison, the first law chancellor of Virginia, ancestor of the two Presidents of that name, and through his mother he was the lineal descendant of Col. William Ball, grandfather of General Washington. At fourteen he was prepared for the University of Virginia, but was too young to enter. It was intimated that he would be made an exception as to the age for admission, but his friends thought it inadvisable to enter at such an early age. He continued his studies in Staunton until he was sixteen, entered the University, and took the degree of master of arts in two years, with additional tickets—mixed mathematics, German and Spanish. He continued his studies while in camp. A gentleman relates that calling on him he found Colonel Fagan in his tent waiting for Colonel Thompson. Colonel Fagan pointed to a number of books on the table and said: "See that pile of books on German and French military tactics? Thompson has mastered them all."

On leaving the university he was made Professor of Mathematics at Kenyon College, Ohio. The climate not suiting him he went to South America as secretary to Captain Hull, of the *St. Lawrence,* and on his return was elected president of St. John's College, Little Rock. He was most successful in building up the school, and when the war broke out no college in the country had a fairer prospect of success nor offered a nobler sacrifice on the altar of country. Colonel Thompson's professors were men of the highest character and attainments, and of his boys has been written: "These boys were flowers of

Southern blood and under arms in war constituted a body of heroes worthy of comparison with those of Thermopylæ" (Parks). Colonel Fellows wrote me that "not one of those boys deserted, showed the white feather, or was court-martialed for any offense whatever." In the fall, before the Battle of Shiloh, Colonel Thompson, thinking camp life demoralizing for his boys, requested to be sent to the South. At the Battle of Shiloh General Johnston wished to locate the enemy and the First Arkansas was ordered to unmask their batteries. Colonel Thompson volunteered to lead the forlorn hope. General Fagan remonstrated, saying it was *his* place and he would not resign it. Colonel Thompson said, "No, General, I will go; you have a wife and children. I have none."* On the march the view was obstructed by a tangle of brushwood, and Colonel Thompson taking a dangerously exposed position tried to discover the enemy's whereabouts. Some of his boys begged to take the risk (of sharp-shooters) in his place, but he refused, saying, "I will *lead* but never *send* you into danger." This was his idea of a "sacred trust." As they were standing below him he remarked to one of his officers who had been his companion of many a hunting expedition, "This is different game, Bronaugh, from that we used to fol-

*In June, 1858, he was married to Miss Alice Powers (the eldest daughter of Pike Powers, Esq.) of Staunton, between whom and himself an attachment had existed for years. The same year he accepted the Presidency of St. John's College, Little Rock, an institution established by the Free Masons of Arkansas. While the dark war-cloud was rising over the land, his own life was darkened by the death of his wife, a woman of singularly pure spirit, vigorous intellect and elegant accomplishments, in every way worthy of him. She died in the hope of the Gospel of Christ. The stricken husband bore the blow with manly fortitude and Christian resignation.

low." The battery was unmasked and at the first fire he fell wounded in seven places. As the battle was fought with varying fortunes the field hospital was now with one army, now with the other. Both the Federal surgeons and his own vied with each other in care of him. He was cheerful to the end, saying, "I commend my soul to God; my life I give joyfully to my country."

He wrote the following letter to his father, the night before the battle:

"*Night of April* 4, 1862.

"MY DEAR FATHER:

"I write by the light of our bivouac fires. We expect by God's help a glorious victory tomorrow. If I should not see you again, take the assurance that I trust in God to be prepared for all. Day after to-morrow is my twenty-seventh birthday. Love to all. "Your devoted son,

"JOHN BAKER THOMPSON."

The morning before the battle one of his officers, seeing he had a new uniform, said, "Thompson, you should keep that to receive their surrender in." He smiled and shook his head. After he was wounded he turned to this friend and said, "and they dressed him for his burial." He was buried on the field, under a large tree, his name and rank cut in the bark. After the war, when his remains were removed, the inscription was found as legible as when first placed there. His remains were laid with those of his beloved wife under a monument he had erected to her memory in beautiful Hollywood, where he rests with his comrades who with him died for home and country. The inscription—

Lt.-Col. John Baker Thompson, First Arkansas Regiment, fell while gallantly contesting the field of Shiloh.
"He giveth his beloved sleep."

Thus lived and died the young soldiers of the Confederacy—a generation of civilization destroyed.

"O Liberty, what crimes are committed in thy name!"

OBITUARY

"John Baker Thompson, son of Judge Lucas Powell Thompson, of Staunton, Va., and lieutenant-colonel of the First Arkansas Regiment, fell while gallantly contesting the field of Shiloh. A nobler sacrifice has not been laid on Freedom's altar."—*Richmond Dispatch.*

POEM BY TIMROD

"And thou art gone; grim death has wrapped
Thee in his chilled embrace and stilled
The genial pulses of thy soul;
Hushed the proud throbbings of that breast
And dimmed the calm eye forever
Wont to beam on all so kindly.
Must yearning friendship say farewell,
No more to feel the gladdening thrill
Of sweet communion with thee?
Thy sun of life hath set in all
Its noontide glory, but again
Resplendent it shall rise to shine
Midst scenes more bright and lovely far
Than this cold world of ours.
The path was bright before thee;
Thou hadst garnered up rich store
Of human wisdom; the fond hopes
Of many a loved one hung on thee;
But these, alas! have perished, and
The sweeter hope doth rise that thou
Hast found a fadeless shore where storms
Do wreck not, war doth rage no more.

Many did fall on Shiloh's plain,
Noble the victims offered up,
Red waxed the altar fires, but not
From shrine of Liberty arose
On the air of evening incense
More costly than thy dying breath.
Farewell! no more we'll see thee midst
The gathering throng of heroes; but
When other brighter days shall come
And laurels crown the brows stern fate
Hath spared, and earth's exultant shouts
Intoxicate the champions of
Sweet liberty, our hearts will turn
To think a crown stainless and pure
Doth grace thy sacred head; a crown
Eternal, bright and beautiful.
How shall we miss thee e'en though years
Shall pass away, and others stand
Where thou in glory mightst have stood.
Adieu, for we have loved thee and
Shall mourn thee long. Adieu, we leave
Thee to thy peaceful rest which naught
Can break; thy wakeless, dreamless sleep.
The battle roar, fit requiem to
Thy gallant spirit, strikes not on
The palsied ear now drinking in
The choirings of bright cherubim."

"THE MAGNIFICENT FIRST ARKANSAS REGIMENT OF INFANTRY"

"The First Arkansas Regiment enlisted directly into the Confederate Army as originally organized, and was composed of the following staff officers: James F. Fagan, colonel; James C. Monroe, lieutenant-colonel; John Baker Thompson, major; Frank Bronaugh, adjutant. On the formation of the regiment it was moved to Lynchburg, Va., where it was mustered into the Confederate service on the 26th day of May, 1861, and surrendered on the 27th day of April, 1865. The regiment was in seventeen general engagements, skirmished 200 days, and marched over 9,000 miles. At the time of its organization it numbered 1,100 men, besides being recruited several times. At the close of the war 39 remained, 32 were prisoners, and 7 surrendered at Appomattox. The loss of the regiment at Shiloh reached the aggregate of 364 killed, wounded and missing. Major J. W. Colquitt was severely wounded late in the action, so seriously that he was obliged to go to his home in Georgia on leave. The train on which he traveled was captured by the Yankees at Huntsville, Ala., but he escaped, although on crutches, and made his way safely home. When he recovered from his wound he rejoined his regiment as its colonel (Colonel Fagan being promoted), and commanded it until he was desperately wounded at Atlanta July 26, 1864, losing his right foot; after which he was put on post duty at West Point, Miss., where he remained until the surrender.

"From the 'Life of General Albert Sidney Johnston,' the Confederate commanding general in the Battle of Shiloh, I quote the following:

" 'The First Arkansas Regiment, of which John Baker Thompson was lieutenant-colonel, was in its second engagement when he met a soldier's fate April 6, 1862, on this hard-fought field—one of the most memorable battles, in some respects, of this or any other age.'

"On the right of the regiment, dauntlessly leading the advance, fell Lieut.-Col. John Baker Thompson, mortally wounded, pierced with seven balls. His loss no one can feel as sensibly as myself. Like Havelock, he united the graces of religion to the valor of the soldier.

"With much respect,

"Very truly,

(Signed) "JAS. F. FAGAN,

"Col. Commanding 1st Ark. Regt."

APPENDIX

Appendix I

THE CAUSE FOR WHICH THEY FOUGHT

"The Southern States proclaimed the right of nationalities, demanded their independence, and proved their earnestness and unanimity by arguments that were far more unequivocal than doubtful plebiscite. For four long years they defended their cause on the battlefield with heroic courage, against overwhelming odds and at the sacrifice of everything that men most desire. American and indeed European writers are accustomed to speak of the heroism of the American colonies in repudiating imperial taxation and asserting and achieving their independence against all the force of Great Britain. But no one who looks carefully into the history of the American Revolution, who observes the languor, the profound divisions, the frequent pusillanimity, the absence of all strong and unselfish enthusiasm that were displayed in great portions of the revolted colonies and their dependence for success on foreign assistance, will doubt that the Southern States in the war of secession exhibited an incomparably higher level of courage, tenacity and self-sacrifice. But it was encountered with an equal tenacity and with far greater resources, and after a sacrifice of life unequalled in any war since the fall of Napoleon, the North succeeded in crushing the revolt and establishing its authority over the vanquished South. LECKY."

APPENDIX II

THEIR PRESIDENT

"Jefferson Davis was born at beautiful Fairfield, Ky., June 3, 1808. He was destined to be the leader of a liberty-loving people whose courage and fidelity to principle and sacrifices to be made for liberty's cause would write upon the pages of American history a story that for all time would command the admiration of the world.

"As a leader of the Southern people, as President of the Confederate States, Jefferson Davis was made to suffer for the people as no other leader ever was that modern history records. His purity of private character, his patriotism, his love of justice and truth, his eminent ability as a statesman made him not only a leader of men, but gave him rank as the peer of any man of his day. His gentle manner, his courtesy to his humblest fellow-man, his personal courage and rare judgment endeared him to our people. We loved him for his sterling virtues, we loved him as a comrade and friend. Today his bitterest foes are compelled to concede that he was honest and courageous in his life's work. Mr. Davis was not only a statesman; he was a soldier of conceded ability and won his spurs upon many Mexican battlefields in the cause of the Government whose persecution of him was cruel and inhuman.

"When the South was forced to withdraw from the union of States, we turned as one man to Jefferson Davis as our leader. A statesman was needed as well as a trained soldier; a man with the will to do, the soul to dare. In Mr. Davis we found the ideal man to guide the destinies of the infant republic, organize her civil departments, and steer her clear of the rocks and breakers of the times. By common consent of all the delegates of the seceding States assembled in convention at Montgomery, Alabama, in 1861, Mr. Davis was chosen Provisional President of the Confederate States of America. In 1862 he was elected by the votes of the whole people of the South Constitutional President of the Confederate States.

"Positively Mr. Davis did not seek the position—the position sought him. After the State of Mississippi seceded from the Union, Mr. Davis was appointed by the Governor commander-in-chief of the State forces, and he was as much astonished as man could be when the Montgomery convention chose him President. It is absurd for the writers and historians of the North to insist, as they do, that Mr. Davis was the choice of the politicians and not of the whole people of the South. He was absolutely the people's choice. The movement of the South in 1861 was sudden, and it was vast, it is true, but it was not the work of politicians; it was the action of a people who had been rudely awakened from their dream of security. A great danger presented itself to the whole South. A necessity for quick action confronted the people. Their liberty and happiness were threatened by the fanatics who had gotten control of the Government power, and these people left the South but one course, that was separation from the union of States."

Gen. Robert E. Lee said of President Davis to a lady asking him a question: "You can always say there are few who could have done better than Mr. Davis. I know *none* who could have done as well."—("Life and Letters of General Lee," by R. E. Lee, Jr.)

JEFFERSON DAVIS'S OPINION OF LEE

"After the close of the war, while I was in prison and Lee was on parole, we were both indicted on a charge of treason; but, in hot haste to get in their work, the indictment was drawn with the fatal omission of an overt act. General Grant interposed in the case of General Lee, on the ground that he had taken his parole and that he was, therefore, not subject to arrest. Another grand jury was summoned, and a bill was presented against me alone, and amended by inserting specifications of overt acts. General Lee was summoned as a witness before that grand jury, the object being to prove by him that I was responsible for certain things done by him during the war. I was in Richmond, having been released by virtue of the writ of *habeas corpus*. General Lee met me very soon after having given his testimony before the grand jury, and told me that to the inquiry whether he had not, in the specified cases, acted under my orders, he said that he had always consulted me when he had the opportunity, both on the field and elsewhere; that after discussion, if not before, we had always agreed, and therefore he had done with my consent and approval only what he might have done if he had not consulted me, and that he accepted the full responsibility for his acts. He said he had endeavored to present the matter as distinctly as he could, and looked up to see what effect he was producing upon the grand jury. Immediately before him sat a big black negro, whose head had fallen back on the rail of the bench he sat on; his mouth was wide open, and he was fast asleep. General Lee pleasantly added that, if he had had any vanity as an orator, it would have received a rude check.

"The evident purpose was to offer to Lee a chance to escape by transferring to me the responsibility for overt acts. Not only to repel the suggestion, but unequivocally to avow his individual responsibility, with all that, under existing circumstances, was implied in this, was the highest reach of moral courage and gentlemanly pride. Those circumstances were exceptionally perilous to him. He had been indicted for treason; the United States President had vindictively threatened to make treason odious; the dregs of society had been thrown to the surface; judicial seats were held by political adventurers; the United States judge of the Virginia district had answered to a committee of Congress that he could pack a jury so as to convict Davis or Lee—and it was under such surroundings that he met the grand jury and testified as stated above. Arbitrary power might pervert justice and trample on right, but could not turn the knightly Lee from the path of honor and truth.

"Descended from a long line of illustrious warriors and statesmen, Robert Edward Lee added new glory to the name he bore, and, whether measured by a martial or an intellectual standard, will compare favorably with those whose reputation it devolved upon him to sustain and emulate.

"JEFFERSON DAVIS."

APPENDIX III.

CHARLES FRANCIS ADAMS'S TRIBUTE TO LEE

"Confederate Veterans of New York:

"At this banquet, your annual commemoration of Robert E. Lee, I am asked to respond to a sentiment in his honor, and, without reservation, I do so; for, as a Massachusetts man, I see in him exemplified those lofty elements of personal character which, typifying Virginia at her highest, made Washington possible. The possession of such qualities by an opponent cannot but cause a thrill of satisfaction from the sense that we also, as foes no less than as countrymen, were worthy of him, and of those whom he typified. It was a great company, that old, original thirteen; and in the front rank of that company Virginia, Massachusetts, and South Carolina stood conspicuous. So I recognize a peculiar fellowship between them—the fellowship of those who have both contended shoulder to shoulder, and fought face to face.

"This, however, is of the past. Its issues are settled, never to be raised again. But, no matter how much we may discuss the rights and the wrongs of a day that is dead,—its victories and defeats,—one thing is clear beyond dispute—victor and vanquished, Confederate and Unionist, the descendants of those who, between 1861 and 1865, wore the gray and of those who wore the blue, enter as essential and as equal factors into the national life which now is, and in future is to be. Not more so Puritan and Cavalier in England, the offspring of Cromwell and the children's children of Strafford. With us, as with them, the individual exponents of either side became in time common property, and equally the glory of all.

"So I am here this evening, as I have said, a Massachusetts man as well as a member of the Loyal Legion, to do honor to the memory of him who was chief among those once set in array against us. Of him, what shall I say? Essentially a soldier, as a soldier Robert E. Lee was a many-sided man. I might speak of him as a strategist; but of this aspect of the man, enough has perhaps been said. I might refer to the respect, the confidence and love with which he inspired those under his command. I might dilate on his restraint in victory; his resource and patient endurance in the face of adverse fortune; the serene dignity with which he, in the end, triumphed over defeat. But, passing over all these well-worn themes, I shall confine myself to that one attribute of his which, recognized in a soldier by an opponent, I cannot but regard as his surest and loftiest title to enduring fame. I refer to his humanity in arms, and his scrupulous regard for the most advanced rules of civilized warfare. * * * As an American, as an ex-soldier of the Union, as one who did his best in honest, even fight to destroy that fragment of the army of the Confederacy to which he found himself opposed, I rejoice that no hatred attaches to the name of Lee. Reckless of life to attain the legitimate ends of war, he sought to mitigate its horrors. Opposed to him at Gettysburg, I here, forty years later, do him justice. No more creditable order ever issued from a commanding general than that formulated and signed at Chambersburg by Robert E. Lee as, toward the close of June, 1863, he advanced on a war of invasion. 'No greater disgrace,' he then declared, 'can befall the army and through it our whole people, than the perpetration of barbarous outrages upon the innocent and defenseless. Such proceedings not only disgrace the perpetrators and all connected with them, but are subversive of the discipline and efficiency of the army, and destructive of the ends of our movement. It must be remembered that we make war only on armed men.' Lee did not, like Tilly and Mélac, exhort his followers to kill and burn, and burn and kill; and again kill and burn—to make war hell. He did not proclaim that he wanted no prisoners. He did not enjoin it upon his soldiers as a duty to cause the people of Pennsylvania to remember they had been there. I thank Heaven he did not. He at least, though a Confederate in arms, was still an American, and not a Tilly nor a Mélac.

"And here, as a soldier of the Army of the Potomac, let me bear my testimony to such of the Army of Northern Virginia as may now be present. While war at best is bad, yet its necessary and unavoidable badness was not in that campaign enhanced. In scope and spirit Lee's order was observed, and I doubt if a hostile force ever advanced into an enemy's country, or fell back from it in retreat, leaving behind less cause of hate and bitterness than did the Army of Northern Virginia in that memorable campaign which culminated at Gettysburg. Because he was a soldier, Lee did not feel it incumbent upon him to proclaim himself a brute, or to exhort his followers to brutality.

"I have paid my tribute. One word more and I have done. Some six months ago, in a certain academic address at Chicago, I called to mind the fact that a statue of Oliver Cromwell now stood in the yard of Parliament House in London, close to that historic hall of Westminster from the roof of which his severed head had once looked down. * * * I asked why should it not also in time be so with Lee? Why should not his effigy, erect on his charger, and wearing the insignia of his Confederate rank, gaze from his pedestal across the Potomac at the Virginia shore, and his once dearly loved home at Arlington? He, too, is one of the precious possessions of what is an essential factor in the nation that now is, and is to be.

"My suggestion was met with an answer to which I would now make reply. * * * The thing was pronounced impossible.

"Now let me here explain myself. I never supposed that Robert E. Lee's statue in Washington would be provided for by an appropriation from the national treasury. I did not wish it. I do not think it fitting. Indeed, I do not rate high statues erected by act of Congress and paid for by public money. They have small significance. Least of all would I suggest such a one in the case of Lee. Nor was it so with Cromwell. His effigy is a private gift, placed where it is by Parliament. So, when the time is ripe, should it be with Lee—and the time will come. When it does come, the effigy, assigned to its place merely by an act of the Congress of a reunited people, should bear some such inscription as this:—

"ROBERT EDWARD LEE
erected by the contributions
of those who,
wearing the Blue, or wearing the Gray,
recognize Brilliant Military Achievements,
and honor Lofty Character
evinced by
Humanity in War
and by
Devotion and Dignity in Defeat."